MODERN WAR

THE AFGHAN WAR

Men of 45 Commando being air lifted by a Chinook helicopter.

MODERN WARFARE

THE AFGHAN WAR

Operation Enduring Freedom
2001–2014

Anthony Tucker-Jones

Pen & Sword
MILITARY

First published in Great Britain in 2014 by
PEN & SWORD MILITARY
an imprint of
Pen & Sword Books Ltd,
47 Church Street,
Barnsley,
South Yorkshire
S70 2AS

ISBN 978 178303 020 0

Typeset by CHIC GRAPHICS

Printed and bound in India by Replika Press Pvt. Ltd.

Pen & Sword Books Ltd incorporates the imprints of Pen & Sword
Archaeology, Atlas, Aviation, Battleground, Discovery, Family
History, History, Maritime, Military, Naval, Politics, Railways, Select, Social
History, Transport, True Crime, and Claymore Press, Frontline Books,
Leo Cooper, Praetorian Press, Remember When, Seaforth Publishing
and Wharncliffe.

For a complete list of Pen & Sword titles please contact
Pen & Sword Books Limited
47 Church Street, Barnsley, South Yorkshire, S70 2AS, England
E-mail: enquiries@pen-and-sword.co.uk
Website: www.pen-and-sword.co.uk

Contents

Preface

Pen & Sword's Modern Warfare series is designed to provide a visual account of the defining conflicts of the late twentieth and early twenty-first centuries. These include Operations Desert Storm, Iraqi Freedom and Enduring Freedom. A key characteristic of all three, fought by coalitions, is what has been dubbed 'shock and awe' whereby superior technology, air supremacy and overwhelming firepower ensured complete freedom of manoeuvre on the ground in the face of a numerically stronger enemy. The focus of this series is to explain how military and political goals were achieved so swiftly and decisively.

Another aspect of modern warfare is that it is conducted in the full glare of the international media. This is a trend that first started during the Vietnam War and to this day every aspect of a conflict is visually recorded and scrutinized. Such visual reporting often shapes public perceptions of conflict to a far greater extent than politicians or indeed generals.

All the photos in this book, unless otherwise credited, were issued by the US Department of Defense and the UK's Ministry of Defence at the time of the conflict. The author and the publishers are grateful for the work of the various forces' combat photographers.

Introduction

The Unholy Trinity

The war on terror reached a watershed in 2014 with the withdrawal of the North Atlantic Treaty Organisation (NATO)-led International Security Assistance Force from Afghanistan. After ten long years the international community decided to bring to an end its efforts to establish security and stability in the war-torn country. What had started as an act of punishment against those who support global terrorism had rapidly turned into a very costly and drawn out counter-insurgency war.

Despite the huge technological lead and overwhelming firepower of the International Security Assistance Force (ISAF), it was never able to defeat completely the elusive Taliban, who simply fled to their sanctuaries in the mountains of Afghanistan and neighbouring Pakistan. The tough Taliban fighters used much the same weaponry as the Mujahideen had during their decade-long struggle against the invading Soviet army. Washington's response to the spreading insurgency was much the same. Having initially defeated a poorly equipped conventional enemy with 'shock and awe', it sought to repeat the process by confronting the insurgents with massive troop surges and 'shock and awe' strategies designed to clear Afghanistan's provinces and extend the rule of the Afghan government in Kabul.

The trigger for Operation Enduring Freedom (OEF) occurred on 11 September 2001. The world had watched in horror when jihadist terrorists crashed two airliners into New York's World Trade Center, one into the Pentagon and a fourth came down in rural Pennsylvania en route to who knows where.

More traditional airline hostage taking now saw the aircraft itself become an effective weapon in asymmetrical warfare. Al-Qaeda terrorists signalled that no longer was diverting an aircraft and or blowing it up on the tarmac sufficient to further their ends. The airliner had become a horrific force multiplier. The fear and disgust caused by 9/11 was palpable and the spectre of such outrages haunted every major city around the world. Osama bin Laden, leader of al-Qaeda, was immediately named as Washington's prime suspect and he was in hiding in Afghanistan.

Drugs, war and terrorism were the unholy trinity that bought the American-led air war crashing down upon the Taliban regime in Afghanistan in early October 2001.

Within the space of a month British and American air power under OEF brought the Taliban to their knees and facilitated the Northern Alliance's capture of Kabul. After three months military action ended five years of hated Taliban rule and scattered the al-Qaeda terrorist organisation.

Al-Qaeda's supporters trapped in Tora Bora proved not so much a resilient guerrilla army, but demoralised terrorists whose plans for global mayhem had gone awry. However, it was to take two weeks of fighting and relentless American bombing to clear the caves and tunnels, finally ending al-Qaeda's foothold in Afghanistan.

The Battle of Tora Bora proved not such much a dramatic last stand by the militants, but more of a desperate rearguard action to distract the Coalition while senior members of the Taliban and al-Qaeda leadership including Osama bin Laden and Ayman al-Zawahiri escaped. What followed was a ten-year campaign to defend Afghanistan from a resurgent and vengeful Taliban intent on creating chaos.

Although the Taliban were swiftly ousted, bin Laden slipped the net for ten long years. Additionally, the West optimistically assumed it could impose democracy on what is essentially a failed state that has never functioned under an effective unitary authority. Historically, Afghanistan's competing interests only pay lip service to whoever is sitting in Kabul, as the Russians discovered during their decade-long involvement with the country in the 1980s.

While al-Qaeda suffered notable leadership losses in Afghanistan, it was unclear whether its international supporters depended upon its survival to function, thereby leaving a residual international threat. Encouraged by the swift resolution in Afghanistan, many countries with long-standing terrorist problems made fresh attempts to address them and there was a greater level of support for the Middle East peace process. At the same time the US developed a broader anti-terrorist strategy focusing on al-Qaeda links and networks in such countries as the Philippines, Somalia, Uzbekistan and Yemen. In a worldwide clamp down some 500 terrorist suspects were arrested.

The Battle of Tora Bora proved a salutary lesson that terrorist havens around the world would no longer be tolerated and that counter-terrorism had become the dominant feature of warfare in the twenty-first century. However, the war on terror has since proved to be a long, hard struggle. In the years following the fall of the Taliban, Britain's Operation Veritas turned into a rolling commitment known as Operation Herrick. Since then, under the command and control of NATO, the ISAF slowly expanded its area of control out from Kabul to extend the authority of President Hamid Karzai's government.

The Afghan army has a chequered history. It has struggled to define a sense of national identity and maintain the loyalty of its recruits through a series of wars.

During the Soviet invasion in 1979 elements of an Afghan armoured regiment bravely resisted attempts by Soviet special forces to take control of the Presidential Palace in Kabul.

On the whole, however, vast sections of the Afghan army simply melted away and ended up joining the resistance. Those forces that remained loyal to the authorities in Kabul always played second fiddle to the Soviet army. After the invasion only the Afghan commando brigade fought with distinction alongside the Soviets against the revolt by the Mujahideen. However, these special forces were soon exhausted by the constant tempo of operations against the rebels. Just before the Soviet withdrawal the operation to relieve the key border town of Khost was supposed to have been Afghan led, but ended up requiring Soviet special forces to break the deadlock.

Following Moscow's withdrawal a decade later, the Afghan army bolstered by vast quantities of Soviet armaments heroically held out against the rebels for a number of years. Gradually, though, as supplies ran low, isolated garrisons were picked off and eventually the Mujahideen triumphed and rolled into Kabul. Former Afghan generals and their troops then fought alongside the Mujahideen as they sort to stave off the Taliban.

In particular, it was difficult to overcome tribal and regional ties which took precedence over loyalty to Kabul. Afghanistan's patchwork quilt of different ethnic groups inevitably compounded the problem. The majority Pashtun and Tajik peoples often find themselves at loggerheads with the smaller groupings such as the Hazara, Uzbek and Turkmen. The Pashtuns, known as Pathans by the British army, have a fierce fighting reputation. Likewise, the country has two official languages Pashto and Dari, but dozens of others are spoken. Sunni Muslims are in the majority, which puts the Shia at a disadvantage. Afghanistan itself is physically divided by the mountain chain that runs east–west towards Iran. For a decade the Afghan National Army (ANA) struggled to find its feet.

On 7 October 2011 Britain marked the tenth anniversary of its involvement in the war on terror in Afghanistan. At the time the British government's commitment to OEF seemed appropriate. The Taliban had refused to hand over Osama bin Laden following the 9/11 terrorist attacks in the US and Afghanistan was a safe haven for a vast array of terror groups. By 2014, though, Britain and the US had endured enough bloodshed and withdrew.

Chapter One

War is Declared

Operation Enduring Freedom was born after British Prime Minister Tony Blair met with President George W. Bush at the White House on 20 September 2001. Following the first news of the 9/11 attacks Blair was convinced it was the work of al-Qaeda and his immediate response was to offer his support to the US. Britain's intelligence chiefs, notably the heads of the Security Service, Secret Intelligence Service and the Government Communications Headquarters, immediately flew to Washington for urgent talks with their counterparts.

Blair's intelligence advice was that bin Laden was the only one capable of such an attack, and he did not believe any rogue states were involved. In addition, Blair was of the view that simply removing bin Laden from the picture would not be enough – he was right as militant Islam was already much too well established around the world. To some the spread of Saudi Wahhabism, which preaches a return to the pure and orthodox practice of the 'fundamentals' of Islam, was seen as a threat to more moderate Muslim beliefs. Blair wanted a long-term strategy for dealing with Islamic fundamentalism, but what he really meant was Islamic militancy. Bush told Blair that the focus would be Osama bin Laden and Afghanistan's Taliban government. Washington demanded that the Taliban hand over bin Laden immediately – they refused.

The very day after 9/11 Bush declared the attacks on the American homeland as acts of war and requested Congress provide the resources to fight the terrorists wherever they might be in the shape of $20 billion. Congress's response was to approve double this sum. The following day US Secretary of State, Colin Powell, confirmed that Osama bin Laden, believed to be hiding in Afghanistan, was a key suspect.

Behind the scenes the American government had been expecting such a spectacular attack for almost ten years. In addition, Blair was very familiar with Islamic militant groups because Britain had tolerated fundraising offices in London for so long and had a growing awareness of al-Qaeda.

Bin Laden's complicity in the planning of 9/11 was confirmed by a videotape made in January 2000 (obtained by the *Sunday Times*). This showed 9/11 hijackers Mohammed Atta and Ziad Jarrah at bin Laden's HQ at Tarnak Farms, near Kandahar airport, in Afghanistan. In total the 9/11 attacks are estimated to have killed 2,973 people, some

2,602 at the World Trade Center, 125 at the Pentagon and 40 in Pennsylvania; 15 hijackers were from Saudi Arabia, 2 from the United Arab Emirates, 1 from Egypt and 1 from Lebanon.

Bin Laden later said, 'We calculated in advance the number of casualties from the enemy, who would be killed based on the position of the tower. We calculated that the floors that would be hit would be three or four floors. I was the most optimistic of them all . . '. US forces discovered a videotape recorded in November 2001 containing this statement by bin Laden, which was made during a meeting with a Saudi supporter in Jalalabad, Afghanistan. With these words he became America's public enemy number one. What most Americans did not realise was that Washington had spent the last four years trying to kill him.

On that fateful day the first aircraft struck the World Trade Center north tower at 8.47am local time, the second smashed into the south tower 16 minutes later. By 10.30am before the world's media both towers had collapsed into a mass of shattered glass, concrete and steel. Manhattan disappeared into a pall of choking smoke and dust centred on what become dubbed 'Ground Zero', a term normally associated with the impact of a nuclear warhead. New Yorkers covered in choking dust staggered about their city in a daze of incomprehension and terror.

Less than an hour after the first New York attack, just outside Washington the third hijacked aircraft flew into the south-west side of the Pentagon at 9.38am. The attack was so precise many initially though the building had been hit by a missile. About 25 minutes later the fourth aircraft came down in Pennsylvania after the intervention of the passengers who had sought unsuccessfully to regain control of the aircraft.

The United Nations had acted against Afghanistan, or more precisely the Taliban, for harbouring bin Laden and those implicated in the attacks on the Khobar Towers in Saudi Arabia, the US embassies in Africa, the USS *Cole* off Yemen and an earlier attempt to blow up the World Trade Center during the 1990s. A UN Security Council resolution came into effect in November 1999, banning the Afghan carrier Ariana Airlines from operating overseas and freezing Taliban overseas assets.

Throughout the late 1990s the Central Intelligence Agency (CIA) had been instructed to capture bin Laden using lethal force if necessary. This lead to confusion over President Clinton's true intentions. He argued he wanted bin Laden dead, the CIA countered they were only instructed to capture him. UN Security Council resolution 1333 of 19 January 2001 followed a month's grace to allow the Taliban to comply with demands to hand over bin Laden and close down the terrorist training camps. The Taliban's acquiescence of the presence of al-Qaeda and its complicity in the country's drug trade had ensured Afghanistan remained a pariah state.

Since the end of 2000 the UN had been demanding that Afghanistan stop giving sanctuary to bin Laden and his al-Qaeda terrorist organisation. However, 9/11 was a harsh reminder of the failure of the world to act effectively in concert against the growing threat posed by extensive international Islamic terrorist networks. An attack of this magnitude and visibility against air travel simply could not be ignored. After 9/11 Washington would have happily seen him dead and by this stage armed aerial drones were available to help pinpoint and kill terrorist leaders.

Initially, al-Qaeda had planned hijacking a total of ten planes with the intention of crashing them into targets on both coasts of the US. The targets would have included nuclear power plants and tall buildings in California and Washington State. This could have been devastating, but as it was just four planes had the desired effect. The US asked itself what had it done to inspire such an act of hatred by militant members of Islam? The international community was also put on notice that such outrages would become more commonplace in the world's capitals over the next decade.

Following 9/11 the international community immediately rallied to the US. The very next day UN Security Council resolution 1368 and General Assembly resolution 56/1 called for immediate international cooperation to bring the perpetrators to justice. They also called for much broader cooperation against global terrorism and this was followed on 28 September 2001 by UN Security Council resolution 1373. Enacted under Chapter VII of the UN Charter, it required every member state to undertake seventeen measures against all those who support, directly or indirectly, acts of terrorism.

For the very first time the NATO invoked its mutual defence clause on 2 October 2001, whereby an attack on a member state is considered an attack on all. Five days later the American and British-led Coalition began systematic air attacks on the Taliban. At the same time, American forces tried to kill Osama bin Laden, his deputy Ayman al-Zawahiri, Khalid Shaik Mohammed (architect of 9/11) and Mullah Omar, leader of the Taliban. The al-Qaeda and Taliban hit list was much longer than this, but they were the ones that really mattered and the intelligence community naively hoped that by decapitating al-Qaeda the threat would somehow vanish.

This was too little too late, and 9/11 was in fact the culmination of a decade of steadily spreading militant Islam not the start. Memories were short, for few beyond the intelligence and law-enforcement agencies recalled Ramzi Yousef's dramatic, if ill-fated, truck bomb attack on the World Trade Center on 26 February 1993, which heralded the transnational jihad against the US. The bomb tore through five sublevels near the north tower killing six and injuring over a thousand. It took over a year and a half to restore the damaged complex. His attack-predated bin Laden's declaration of war on the American homeland by three-and-a-half years. In that time militant Islam's rise had gone unchecked.

The US Special Operations Command was granted a budget increase of almost 50 per cent with $250 million being spent on Predator and another $610 million on the Global Hawk unmanned aerial vehicles or drones in order to step up the so-called war on terror. After 9/11 the CIA's counter-terrorist efforts came under the scrutiny of a joint inquiry conducted by the US Senate Select and House Permanent Select Committees on Intelligence. To add to the indignity the CIA's Office of Inspector General was then required to endorse the inquiry's scathing findings.

Damningly, the joint inquiry concluded that before 9/11 neither the US government nor the US intelligence community had a comprehensive strategy for dealing with al-Qaeda. The view was that the Director General Central Intelligence 'was either unwilling or unable to marshal the full range of IC resources necessary to combat the growing threat to the United States'. In light of the evidence the Office of Inspector General had little choice but to agree with these findings.

In particular, coordination failures between the CIA and the National Security Agency were identified. The latter was reluctant to share its signals intelligence with the CIA, which hampered the Counterterrorism Center's efforts against al-Qaeda. It likewise stymied coordination between the CIA and US military.

The US military did not escape criticism either. The Pentagon was censured for being reluctant to conduct operations in Afghanistan or support or take part in CIA operations against al-Qaeda prior to 9/11. It was noted that one of the reasons cited for this was the CIA's failure to provide adequate intelligence to support such operations. As a result, the US Defense Department felt it could not put troops on the ground in Afghanistan or conduct cruise-missile attacks on bin Laden-related sites, over and beyond the August 1998 strikes in Afghanistan and Sudan. Disagreements over replacing lost predator drones also needlessly hampered collaboration between the CIA and American military.

The US government's inquiry concluded 'that the CIA was reluctant to seek authority to assassinate bin Laden and averse to taking advantage of ambiguities in the authorities it did receive that might have allowed it more flexibility'. Although the US government wanted bin Laden dead as early as August 1998, it had not removed the ban on assassination and did not provide clear direction or indeed authorisation to the CIA.

This collective intelligence failure meant that American efforts against al-Qaeda before 9/11 were insufficient and ill-coordinated. In the confusion al-Qaeda planned and then executed the 9/11 attacks despite repeated warnings that such a strike was possible against the US heartland. After 9/11 the US found itself at war in Afghanistan and it was not until ten years later that Osama bin Laden was finally run to ground hiding out in the city of Abbottabad, Pakistan.

The man who started it all, Osama bin Laden. A veteran of the Soviet-Afghan War, he and his supporters began to target American interests throughout the 1990s in protest at the American military presence in Saudi Arabia following the Gulf War.

The United Nations HQ in New York. From the end of 2000 the UN had been demanding the Taliban stop giving sanctuary to bin Laden and his terrorist organisation al-Qaeda.

In 1996 bin Laden declared Holy War on American forces in Saudi Arabia. That year al-Qaeda-linked terrorists blew up Khobar Towers in Saudi Arabia killing nineteen American servicemen. The year before five American military advisers had been killed in a bombing in Riyadh.

The attacks continued to escalate and spread around the world. On 7 August 1998 2 massive truck bombs destroyed the American embassies in Kenya and Tanzania killing 252 and wounding another 5,000.

In an audacious attack suicide bombers blew a hole in the side of the USS *Cole* while in Aden harbour, Yemen on 12 October 2000.

In 2001 bin Laden and his supporters laid the foundations for a devastating attack on the twin towers of the World Trade Center in Manhattan, New York. The World Trade Center covered 16 acres and included five buildings in addition to the twin towers, plus a plaza and six underground levels. This was the work place of around 50,000 people employed by 430 companies from all over the world. In addition, it attracted tens of thousand of visitors every day. The formal dedication ceremony occurred in 1973 after initial construction commenced in 1966.

At 8.47am on the morning of 11 September 2001 al-Qaeda terrorists crashed American Airlines Flight 11 into the north tower of the World Trade Center. Catching stunned workers and rescuers by surprise, United Airlines Flight 175 hit the south tower 16 minutes later and exploded on impact.

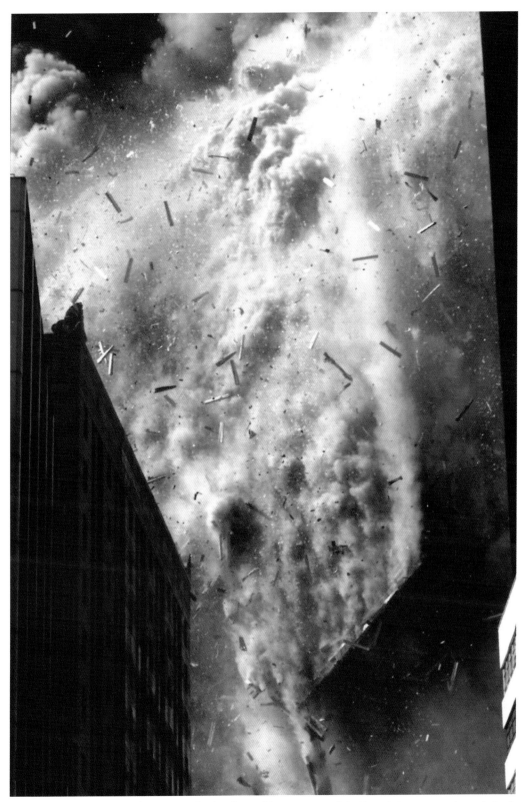

By 10.30am both the blazing towers had collapsed into a mass of shattered glass, concrete and steel.

Manhattan disappeared in a pall of choking smoke and dust following the collapse of the second tower.

New York received such a devastating blow that neither the US nor the international community could let such an act go unpunished.

This photograph was taken on 26 September 2001 and shows the extent of the destruction wrought at Ground Zero where the twin towers once stood. The clear-up was a mammoth task and by the summer of 2002 1.4 million tons of debris had been removed from Ground Zero along with 19,435 body parts. It took over 110,000 truckloads to clear the devastation. More than 11,000 firefighters who responded to 9/11 suffered at least one respiratory symptom within weeks of the attacks.

A third hijacked plane, American Airlines Flight 77, was flown into the Pentagon, the American defence HQ, near Washington DC at 9.38am, less than an hour after the first New York attack.

An aerial view of the gaping hole in the Pentagon. This suicide attack cost the lives not only of the 5 hijackers but also 64 innocent passengers and 125 people in the Pentagon.

This photograph shows where the fire took hold following the impact on the Pentagon.

A fourth plane, United Airlines Flight 93, crashed into a field in Pennsylvania after passengers rushed the hijackers at just after 10am. Investigators were swift to retrieve the flight data recorder near the huge crater carved into the ground by the impact.

The prime suspects for 9/11, Osama bin Laden, leader of al-Qaeda, and his deputy Ayman al-Zawahiri, former leader of Egyptian Islamic Jihad. Despite the massive $25 million bounty, both men eluded capture following 9/11 and the subsequent Operation Enduring Freedom.

Chapter Two

OEF – The Air War

Even before Operation Enduring Freedom, Afghanistan was a very troubled land having endured decades of war. After the Soviet Union's withdrawal from Afghanistan in 1988, its puppet regime eventually collapsed and the country was ruled by a loose confederation of constantly warring Mujahideen factions. They in turn were ousted in 1996 by the devoutly Islamic Taliban movement originating in the city of Kandahar. The former government forces, known as the Northern Alliance (or United Front – representing Afghanistan's Hazara, Tajik, Uzbek and other ethnic minorities), were largely pushed back to an enclave in the north-east of the country protected by the Hindu Kush.

Aiming to punish those responsible for 9/11, President Bush decided to use his air power and special forces to assist the Afghan Northern Alliance to drive the Taliban from Kabul and destroy al-Qaeda's presence once and for all under OEF. This was to involve air strikes, using US Navy (USN) and strategic air assets as well as ship and submarine-launched Tomahawk Land Attack Missiles (TLAMs), to hit terrorist-related facilities, the Taliban's military infrastructure and their field forces.

OEF was directed by US Central Command (CENTCOM) from McDill Air Force Base, Florida. USN aircraft deployed to the region included F-14 Tomcat and F/A-18E/F Super Hornet fighter-bombers and global assets included heavy long-range B-1B, B-2A and B-52H strategic bombers. The US was not able to conduct any regional land-based fighter missions using USAF F-16, as crucially Saudi Arabia and Pakistan refused to allow any attacks to be conducted from their soil. Pakistan's government, with its Pashtun population, brothers of the Pashtun Taliban, had to walk a diplomatic tightrope.

At least 50 per cent of the targets to be bombed were terrorist related. These included training camps, stores, safe houses and mountain hideouts. The camps were used to train Chechens, Kashmiris, Pakistanis, Saudis, Tajiks, Uzbeks, Uighurs and Yemenis. Their services were then exported back to their home countries. The bulk of the terrorist facilities was in the Kabul, Kandahar and Jalalabad areas and belonged to al-Qaeda and the Islamic Movement of Uzbekistan (IMU). In particular Kandahar and Jalalabad were the favoured targets, as these locations were where Osama bin

Laden and his cronies were most likely to have gone to ground. Kandahar was the stronghold of Bin Laden's one-time ally, Taliban leader Mullah Mohammed Omar.

Since its foundation the Taliban Air Force had been active and had flown over 150 sorties during the campaigns to capture the Northern Alliance's capital at Taloqan. However, with the loss of Bagram air base in 1998 it was forced to destroy or disable many of its aircraft during its retreat from the Shomali plain. Against the Coalition air campaign the Taliban Air Force initially had about eight MiG-21, eight Su-22 and about four L-39 light jets plus a few Mi-8/17 helicopters. Most were simply destroyed on the ground in the opening hours of the air attacks.

It is almost impossible to get a consensus on the Taliban and Northern Alliance's tank fleets. However, it would be fair to say that at the time of the American led offensive the Taliban had roughly about 300 tanks, mostly old Soviet-built T-55s and some T-62s, perhaps several hundred tracked BMP-1/2 armoured personnel carriers (APCs), 500 wheeled BTR APCs and some BRDM scout cars. Taliban mobile rocket launchers included some Soviet BM-21 and BM-14, while there were probably no more than a handful of mobile surface-to-surface missile launchers of the Scud and FROG-7a/b variety. The biggest threat to US Air Force emanated from the Taliban's SA-13 mobile surface-to-air missiles. The serviceability of all these vehicles was chronic and it is doubtful that even half were operational.

The goal of the air attacks was to enable the complete destruction of the Taliban regime and the creation of a broad-based successor government under UN auspices. Otherwise drugs, war and terrorism would remain a way of life for another twenty years. In light of their victories over the Northern Alliance and previous experience against the Soviets, the Taliban was not expected to crumble easily. Well before the air strikes started the Afghan economy was already in tatters, and the continuing civil war had prevented any recovery.

The UN identified intensified drug production with the economic, social and political collapse in Afghanistan caused by over two decades of civil war. Afghanistan, a long-established centre of opiate production, after the Taliban's seizure of power in 1996 emerged as the main global supplier of opium. By the late 1990s it accounted for some 75 per cent of the world's opium. It is probable that the trafficking impacted on the Taliban war effort against the Northern Alliance and other factions, as well as its support for regional Islamic guerrilla movements.

Under the Taliban, taxation ceased, foreign investment dried up and there was rampant inflation. The situation was exacerbated in 1998 when Saudi Arabia withdrew essential financial support to the Taliban for harbouring bin Laden. By then he was wanted for various attacks on American interests in Kenya, Saudi Arabia, Tanzania and Yemen.

It was unclear just how far the Taliban relied on these drug revenues to maintain the tempo of their military operations and support for international terrorism. However, it was self-evident from the level of anti-narcotics activity that neighbouring states, such as Iran, were forced to undertake that Afghanistan's narcotics trafficking was a major problem. To the west and east, Iran and Pakistan previously attempted to crack down on drug smuggling across their borders. Ironically, Pakistan's success simply resulted in pushing heroin manufacturing into Afghanistan. Iran in turn expended considerable resources trying to control the well-armed drug warlords.

Profits generated from narcotic exports helped to fund the Afghan civil war. Nevertheless, it remained unclear what percentage of revenues actually reached central Taliban coffers; local Taliban probably benefited the most from drug taxes. The production and smuggling of drugs across Asia also became a vital source of revenue for terrorist and international criminal organisations. This endangered the security and stability of a region threatened by further upheaval.

Beyond Afghanistan's borders to the north, in the Central Asian states, Afghan drug money and organised crime assisted pro-Taliban opposition groups, such as the Islamic Movement of Uzbekistan and the former United Tajik Opposition. Also ethnic Uighurs from China's Xinjiang province (bordering Afghanistan and Tajikistan) were known to have trained in Afghanistan with the IMU. The Uighurs had been agitating against central Chinese authority for years, necessitating a number of large Chinese military operations against them. The IMU was particularly troublesome in the Fergana Valley straddling Tajikistan, Kyrgyzstan and Uzbekistan. Indeed, American bombing was to target the 3,000 IMU fighters supporting the Taliban inside Afghanistan.

Bush's air war opened on 7 October 2001, with B-1 and B-52 bombers flying from the island of Diego Garcia in the Indian Ocean and B-2s flying from Whitman Air Force Base, Missouri. The latter flew on to Diego Garcia after a record 44 hours in the air and six air-to-air refuellings. These bombers were joined by carrier based F-14 and F/A-18 fighter-bombers operating from the aircraft carriers USS *Carl Vinson* and USS *Enterprise*, while some fifty Tomahawks were also launched. The Royal Navy fired two small batches of TLAMs, and the RAF contributed several hundred reconnaissance and tanker refuelling sorties in support. British air support, although small, was significant compared with that of other nations. France's contribution consisted of reconnaissance flights using Mirage IVP and C.160G ELINT (Electronic Intelligence) aircraft and an intelligence-gathering ship. Italy volunteered tactical reconnaissance, air-to-air refuelling, transport aircraft and a naval group. In addition, Turkey announced it would send special forces to train the Northern Alliance.

The key achievement of the intense air attacks was the swift acquisition of air superiority through the destruction of the Taliban's rudimentary air force, air defences and early warning systems. Only isolated SA-13 and man-portable surface-to-air missiles were believed to pose a low-altitude threat. As well as attacking the Taliban's infrastructure, Coalition assets also struck vulnerable dispersal areas, catching exposed Taliban armour in the hills outside Herat. The US Department of Defense released imagery of the air strikes on airfields at Kandahar, Herat and Mazar-e-Sharif, vehicle depots at Kandahar and Pol-e-Charkhi, Herat army barracks and a Kabul radio station, to name but a few targets.

Ironically, initially the air campaign did not greatly affect the Taliban's rudimentary infrastructure or ability to wage war against the Northern Alliance, only its ability to resist Coalition air attack. The Northern Alliance had little in the way of an air force that posed a threat to the Taliban air defences. Until the concentrated attacks on the Taliban's field forces, the degradation of the Taliban's communications was the greatest hindrance to their conduct of the civil war against the Northern Alliance. The American special forces' raids on 19 October 2001 against a command and control facility and an airfield near Kandahar illustrated the Coalition's freedom of operations on the ground. However, it was B-52 carpet-bombing, coupled with Taliban defections and withdrawals, which produced dramatic results and hastened the end of organised resistance. By the close of October air strikes began to shift away from high-profile urban targets toward Taliban front-line positions.

Heavy strikes, including carpet-bombing, were conducted on 31 October against Taliban forces near Bagram, 30 miles north of Kabul. These attacks lasting several hours were the most intense against Taliban front-line positions since the air campaign began. The following day the strategic Taliban garrison at Kala Ata, guarding the approaches to Taloqan, was also attacked. The raid lasted for over 4 hours and windows were allegedly broken up to 15 miles away as a consequence. Attacks also continued in the Kandahar and Mazar-e-Sharif areas. Within a week of this intense bombing the Taliban crumbled first at Mazar-e-Sharif, then Kabul and Jalalabad, their forces in headlong retreat to Kandahar.

US air strikes continued against regrouping Taliban/al-Qaeda forces and their facilities in eastern Afghanistan. These were concentrated in Paktia province against Zhawar Kili, site of the Soviet-backed offensive in 1987. The facility first suffered American air strikes in 1998, in retaliation for the attacks on American embassies in East Africa. According to the US, on 28 December 2001 they bombed a walled compound and bunker associated with the Taliban and al-Qaeda leadership in Paktia province. The media subsequently claimed the attack killed up to 100 innocent civilians.

Sustained raids were conducted on both Zhawar Kili and anti-aircraft defences near the town of Khost. The US feared that Zhawar Kili was going to be another Tora Bora. General Richard Myers of the US Joint Chiefs of Staff said, 'We have found this complex to be very, very extensive. It covers a large area. When we ask people how large they often describe it as huge.' The camp was composed of three separate training areas and two cave complexes. US Marines and special forces moved into the areas after an initial wave of strikes by B-1 and B-52 bombers and carrier-based Navy fighters. They then piled up unexploded ammunition and heavy weapons, which were destroyed by a second series of air attacks.

Despite three attacks on the complex over a four-day period by US aircraft, surviving al-Qaeda leaders repeatedly tried to regroup at a warren of caves and bunkers. One strike on the Zhawar Kili training camp hit tanks and artillery, but it was feared the terrorists remained. The pressure on the Taliban was unrelenting. On 6 January 2002 strikes on Khost and the Zhawar Kili training camp were among 118 sorties flown by American air assets over Afghanistan.

The success of Operation Enduring Freedom hinged on American air power. Photographed in 2001, this formidable-looking US Navy F-14 Tomcat, armed with two AIM 9 Sidewinder air-to-air missiles, a Paveway II Laser Guided GBU-10 2,000-pound bomb and LANTIRN Pod, is preparing for a bombing mission over Afghanistan. As its refuelling probe is visible it is about to conduct air-to-air refuelling.

US Navy F/A-18 Hornets were also instrumental in striking Taliban targets during the opening air attacks. The carrier based F-14 and F/A-18 fighter-bombers operated from the USS *Carl Vinson* and USS *Enterprise*.

The B-2 Spirit multi-role bomber flew from Whitman Air Force Base in Missouri to support the attacks on Afghanistan. They deployed to Diego Garcia in the Indian Ocean after a record 44 hours in the air and six air-to-air refuellings.

The air war opened on 7 October 2001, with B-1 and B-52 bombers (seen here) flying from the island of Diego Garcia. The Cold War warrior B-52 is a much upgraded veteran of the Vietnam War.

The BGM-109 Tomahawk Land Attack Missile. In October 2001, approximately 50 TLAMs struck targets in Afghanistan in the opening hours of the air war. The Royal Navy also fired two small batches. Previously, TLAMs were first fired operationally at Iraqi targets during Operation Desert Storm in 1991, and seven years later they targeted al-Qaeda in Afghanistan and Sudan in retaliation for the bombings of the American embassies in Kenya and Tanzania.

A B-2 Spirit from Whitman Air Force Base, Missouri, conducting air refuelling operations with a KC-135 tanker. The Taliban's rudimentary air defences had no answer to such aircraft which operated with impunity.

A B-2 Spirit soars through the sky after a refuelling. The Taliban had no way of countering such high-altitude aircraft. Only a handful of their Soviet-built SA-13 mobile surface-to-air missiles systems were operable and these were quickly knocked out.

This Ch-47 Chinook has an AH-64 Apache attack helicopter riding 'shotgun'. Supporting the bombers were Close Air Support teams, drawn from the American and British special forces. Operating on the ground with the Afghan opposition forces, they called in air strikes.

Six-man Close Air Support Special Forces A-Teams were inserted to operate alongside the Taliban's nemesis, the Northern Alliance. The special forces equipped with laser designators would pinpoint enemy targets for American air strikes.

A British Chinook dusts off after inserting ground troops. It would be another 5 years before Britain committed any sizeable numbers of troops with the 3,000-strong 3 Commando Brigade.

A RAF tail gunner keeps an eye out for any incoming fire. Heavy machine-gun fire and rocket-propelled grenades constituted the greatest threat to helicopters.

The great wild goose chase for the al-Qaeda leadership. An American Blackhawk helicopter picks up men from 45 Commando during Operation Buzzard in the summer of 2002. Those Taliban not killed or captured scattered into the mountains of Afghanistan and Pakistan.

A British military GR-9 Harrier aircraft conducts a combat patrol over Afghanistan. As the insurgency mounted these aircraft along with RAF Tornados and Army Air Corps Apaches provided valuable close air support for British ground troops.

Chapter Three

OEF – Liberation of Kabul

The key to OEF was driving the Taliban from Kabul – only this would truly herald their defeat. This meant that everywhere they went the Taliban were attacked across the country. The world watched in awe as American air power first chewed up the Taliban's air force, its air defences and then its armour during the campaign.

Although in the wake of 9/11 the US rapidly came to the decision that it wanted the Taliban government and al-Qaeda terrorists ousted, it did not want to do it at the cost of thousands of American troops on the ground. The solution was to use six-man Close Air Support (CAS) Special Forces A-Teams operating alongside the Taliban's nemesis, the Northern Alliance. The special forces, equipped with laser designators, would pinpoint enemy targets for American air strikes.

The US began secretly to insert its CAS teams twelve days after the air campaign opened. The six men of Tiger 01 were infiltrated into northern Afghanistan on 19 October 2001 by two MH-53J Pavelow helicopters of the 160th Special Operations Aviation regiment. In the next few days, liaising with General Fahim's opposition forces, they were involved in efforts to capture Bagram airfield, 45km north of Kabul. This they found defended by some fifty armoured vehicles including tanks, APCs and ZSU-23 Shilka self-propelled Anti Aircraft Artillery (AAA).

Heavy strikes, including B-52 carpet-bombing, were conducted on 31 October against Taliban forces near Bagram. Airstrikes called in by Tiger 01 obliterated everything over a period of 6 hours. The following day the strategic Taliban garrison at Kala Ata, guarding the approaches to Taloqan, was also attacked. The raids lasted for over 4 hours.

Attacks also continued in the south in the Kandahar area and in the north in the Mazar-e-Sharif area. Within a week of this intense bombing the Taliban crumbled first at Mazar-e-Sharif, then Kabul and Jalalabad, and as a result they were in headlong flight to their stronghold at Kandahar. Team Tiger 02 helped General Dostrum capture Mazar-e-Sharif on 9 November 2001, seizing the vital airfield and opening the supply route to Uzebekistan. The team called in strikes directing US Marine Corps FA/-18 and AC-130 Spectre gunships to silence the deadly ZSU-23-4 and T-55s accounting for at least fifty vehicles.

In just a few days during early November the Taliban lost control of much of the country in the face of the Northern Alliance's rapid ground offensive. Also in the prelude to the Northern Alliance's advance, their old enemies the Russians shipped in several hundred tanks and APCs to help them. The dramatic collapse of the Taliban army was due to a combination of American air attacks, defections and an unprecedented level of cooperation between rival anti-Taliban factions. The Northern Alliance quickly gained control of most of the cities north of a line extending from Herat in the far north-west to Kabul in the east.

During the attack on Kabul on 11 November, Tiger 01 team accounted for twenty-nine tanks plus numerous vehicles and artillery pieces. Just three days later it was all over, Kabul had fallen to the Northern Alliance. Tiger 03 directed to help capture the city of Kunduz and destroyed fifty tanks, APCs, AAA and artillery.

Texas 11 helped General Daoud's forces liberate Taloqan, the Northern Alliance's former HQ, and capture Kunduz. On 17 November they called in airstrikes which claimed 5 tanks, 9 BRDM, 1 BTR-70 and 4 trucks. Between 14 and 29 November 2001, their battle-damage assessment included 12 Taliban tanks, 5 ZPU/ZSUs, 3 BMP/BM-21s, 3 BTR-70/BRDMs and 51 lorries. Texas 12, assigned to Hamid Karzi, future interim president, at the town of Tarin Kowt, north of Kandahar, stopped a Taliban counter-attack involving over 80 vehicles including BRDM, and 35 to 45 of these were destroyed.

Within just three months of the air campaign commencing the Taliban government had been routed. Osama bin Laden and al-Qaeda suffered notable losses, particularly at Mazar-e-Sharif and Kunduz. The Taliban troops trapped in Kunduz surrendered, abandoning some 2,000–5,000 foreign supporters to flee or capitulate. After the fall of Kabul the Taliban retired to prepared positions in and around Kandahar, their spiritual heartland in the south. By the end of November, with the collapse of the Taliban field forces, the focus of the air campaign switched to the Kandahar area and Tora Bora near Jalalabad in eastern Afghanistan.

American air attacks were then directed against al-Qaeda terrorist camps in the south of Helmand province. Kandahar surrendered to opposition forces on 7 December 2001, without a fight. The al-Qaeda fighters trapped there, by the peaks and valleys of the 15,400ft White Mountains, had lost most of their heavy equipment. They had nothing with which to shoot back at the opposition forces' exposed tanks perched on the foothills.

Despite the success of the CAS teams, the use of special forces in Afghanistan came in for some criticism. A former Green Beret said, 'All special operations troops depend too much on technology and aerial support . . . The entire campaigns in Afghanistan and Iraq are flawed. Heavy handed and misuse of special operations troops — thus no relationships with locals and no real intelligence.' In reality prior to the arrival of the American special forces much of the Taliban armour and aircraft had already been smashed at the Afghan storage depots and barracks. Nonetheless, the combination of these teams and American air power sealed the fate of the Taliban.

The stunned survivors from the Taliban's armed forces and al-Qaeda fighters, perhaps over 1,000 men, fled to the Tora Bora stronghold high in the White Mountains late in 2001. Their intention was to use the base to conduct hit and run attacks on the Northern Alliance supporting the Coalition or make a last stand if necessary. Moscow's advice to the Coalition was that this complex could prove to be impregnable if the defenders resisted to the last.

It was anticipated that the Tora Bora stronghold would be protected by minefields, ingenious booby traps and defended by Islamic fanatics prepared to resist to the last. The core of the defenders were thought to number 300, of whom half were Arabs and the rest Chechens, Uzbeks, Tajiks and Afghans. However, other estimates put them as strong as 1,500.

Washington decided that it would not deploy its 500 US Marines on standby at Kandahar, but leave it to its special forces and the Eastern Council to clear the caves. On the Pakistani side of the border Pakistan's military kept the Khyber and Bati passes closed to try and prevent any terrorists slipping through undetected and then up into the unruly North West Frontier Province. As many as 2,000 al-Qaeda fighters were thought to have fled towards Pakistan.

British and American special forces were concentrated on suspected terrorist strongholds, particularly Tora Bora, where bin Laden was believed to be hiding. Babrak Khan, a Jalalabad resident who worked as a guard at an Arab base during the 1990s, said, 'I saw Osama in the sixth or seventh truck and behind him were from 100 to 200 vehicles. At the end of the convoy were five armoured vehicles. Arabs from across the city were gathering here, coming from all directions.' It was claimed bin Laden had helped the city's former governor strike a deal with city elders so they could take control until the formation of an interim government. Having done that, he escaped to Tora Bora.

Meanwhile, Taliban leader Mohammed Omar and 500 of his supporters were thought to be besieged in the rugged mountains of the Bagran area, in northern Helmand. While the Tora Bora region was heavily bombed Afghan opposition forces under the Eastern Council started to advance into the area. These troops blocked off all escape routes prior to launching a major offensive on the region following the fall of Kandahar.

American forces inserted into Afghanistan to help with mopping up operations. Marines with the 15th Marine Expeditionary Unit (Special Operations Capable) move to a security position after seizing a Taliban forward-operating base on 25 November 2001. Marines from both the 15th and 26th MEU were deployed to the region in support of Operation Enduring Freedom. While these forces were initially limited in number, American air power paved the way for the sweeping advance of the Northern Alliance.

Fighters of the Northern Alliance and the Eastern Council played a key role in defeating the Taliban. This anti-Taliban fighter is wrapping a bandolier of ammunition for his 7.62mm PKM (Pulemyot Kalashnikova Modernizirovanniy) Kalashinkov machine gun around his body.

Captured Taliban Scud missiles. Much of the Taliban's heavy equipment that was not destroyed in air strikes was simply abandoned.

Flying in support of the advancing Northern Alliance and special forces were USAF AC-130U Hercules 'Spooky' Gunships, operating with the 4th Special Operations Squadron. These were regularly called on by the American CAS Tiger Teams.

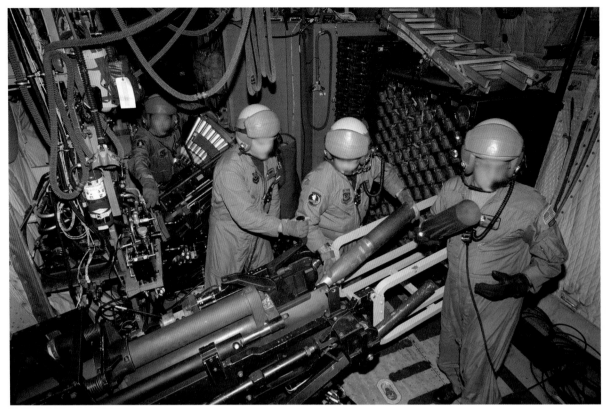

Firepower on the Spooky includes a 105mm Howitzer in the cargo compartment, visible in the foreground, and a 40mm Bofors gun behind it. These can lay down heavy fire support while the aircraft loiters over the target area.

T-55 tanks of the Northern Alliance. The Northern Alliance quickly gained control of most of the cities north of a line extending from Herat in the west to Kabul in the east.

A US Navy F/A-18F Super Hornet aircraft from a Strike Fighter Squadron breaks away from his wingman during a close air support mission in support of coalition forces over Afghanistan. A Paveway laser guided bomb is clearly visible on the right-hand wing.

A Taliban BMP armoured fighting vehicle – this was a left over from the Soviet-Afghan War fought in the 1980s.

The B-52 Stratofortress was used to pound the Taliban's ground positions into oblivion. Within just three months of the air campaign commencing the Taliban had been routed.

Northern Alliance forces gather around a captured Taliban T-55 tank.

Taliban with Grad multiple rocket launchers. Such hardware was highly vulnerable to coalition air attack. The photograph above shows what appears to be a Soviet-built 122mm 12 round Grad-V. The launchers in the image below are the newer 122mm 40 round BM-21 Grad.

Northern Alliance T-55 tanks rolling into Kabul during mid-November 2001. The Taliban proved incapable of holding any of Afghanistan's key cities. Even a last stand in their spiritual homeland in Kandahar failed to materialise.

Another old BM-21 Grad rocket launcher abandoned in the snows of the Afghan winter.

Chapter Four

OEF – The Battle for Tora Bora

US special forces did not arrive in the Tora Bora area until 26 November 2001, partly because it had taken the CIA so long to 'acquire' allies on the ground – no doubt using the US dollar. Colonel John Mulholand, commander of Task Force Dagger, was chaffing at the bit, but first his forces had to get established. The hunt for bin Laden was now stepped up, as reporter Phil Smucker observed firsthand:

> Just across the ravine were two truckloads of plain clothes Green Berets, who were frantically combing the area. They looked, I judged by their appearance, to be belatedly obsessed with an expired mission. Indeed, Col. John Mulholand, commander of Task Force Dagger, which was now engaged in this spelunking exercise, would complain bitterly to me months later about the Promethean mission . . . he would tell me 'This was the great cave hunt which I started to refer to as "Operation Vampire"'. . .

The Tora Bora complex lay south of the city of Jalalabad and west of the famous Khyber Pass, which links Afghanistan with neighbouring Pakistan. Consisting of miles of interconnecting caves and tunnels, it was carved by the anti-Soviet Mujahideen into the side of Ghree Khil Mountain with American and Pakistani sponsorship during the Soviet occupation. Tora Bora first saw action in mid-1981 when a Soviet-led offensive caused widespread destruction though failed to defeat the Mujahideen. The Soviets heavily bombed the stronghold but were unable to root out the resistance fighters. In 2001 Tora Bora was believed to be well provisioned with weapons and food that would allow Osama bin Laden and his supporters to withstand a lengthy siege.

Long-range bombers, tactical jets and helicopter gunships concentrated on one complex near Tora Bora over the space of a few days. The bombing proved successful with the death of many al-Qaeda Arab fighters, including twelve senior personnel in early December. A Daisy Cutter or Big Blue was dropped on a cave near Tora Bora on 9 December. This weapon was previously deployed in Vietnam and the Gulf War. The 15,000-pound BLU-82 was developed in the late 1950s for clearing helicopter landing zones. It was hoped the massive pressure wave cause by the blast would kill suspected al-Qaeda leadership in the cave. The BLU-82 had already been used three times against Taliban and al-Qaeda front lines, but this was the first time it was used against a hard and deeply buried target.

Pakistan stationed 50,000 troops at the Afghan frontier, 8,000 of whom were sent to stop Taliban or al-Qaeda fighters crossing the border. For the first time Pakistan moved the army into the Terah Valley area following reports that Arab suspects might sneak into the tribal territory via Spin Ghar (Pasto for White Mountains) to flee the intense American bombing of Tora Bora.

Haji Mohammad Zaman, senior military commander in the eastern region of Afghanistan and leading the Eastern Council opposition forces, numbering several thousand men, began the laborious task of clearing the Tora Bora Valley. The plan was then to advance on the stronghold itself. First they had to capture the village of Tora Bora and other surrounding hamlets, then clear the Tora Bora forest.

A bitter battle was expected and for the first week the cautious advance was met with some resistance. The Eastern Council's efforts were sluggish because coordination between the various forces was poor. However, al-Qaeda was slowly driven back higher up into the mountains. The opposition forces proceeded to pound the mountains with artillery, mortars, rockets and Russian-supplied T-62 tanks. Al-Qaeda fighters were trapped on all sides by the peaks and valleys of the 15,400ft White Mountains and had lost most of their heavy equipment. They had nothing with which to shoot back at the Eastern Council's exposed tanks perched on the foothills of the White Mountains. In the clear blue skies American B-52s disgorged their heavy munitions in a continuing effort to smash the caves. To the defenders of Tora Bora it must have seemed as if the Americans and Eastern Council forces were trying to smash the very mountains themselves.

After two weeks of constant bombing, the defenders commenced radio negotiations on possible terms. They wanted to surrender to the UN to avoid being handed over to the Americans, but the US would not countenance it. The talks ended and the opposition forces requested the US halt its attacks. The Eastern Council then advanced on the caves still held by Arab al-Qaeda fighters. The mountain paths were narrow and those caves missed by the bombers were difficult to locate. Nonetheless, during the second week of December in the face of varying degrees of resistance Eastern Council forces captured most of al-Qaeda's remaining positions.

The first caves captured revealed evidence of desperate attempts to escape the bombing. Strewn with documents, equipment, ammunition, bloodied rags and weapons, their walls were blackened from fire. The main ground offensive started late on 13 December and the bodies of al-Qaeda supporters posted in machine-gun posts along the ridges were found scattered around the scorched remains of their weapons. Al-Qaeda fighters not killed had fled with no time to plant the feared booby traps.

Phil Smucker recalled:

The battle for Tora Bora was arguably one of the most exciting battles I ever covered as a correspondent. Above us in the clear, blue sky a white Predator drone circled. It buzzed us for five minutes, hovering with its Hellfire missiles like a bird caught in an updraft, then zipped off to unleash its load . . . Within thirty minutes we came out of the gorge and saw the first sign of the vast network of caves and bunkers that is known as Tora Bora. These caves had been the redoubt of . . . al-Qaeda . . .

British and US special forces came under machine-gun and mortar fire as they advanced up the rocky slopes. They fought fierce battles with the survivors for control of the area. Grouped in two or three positions, the last of the terrorist forces were trapped between two parallel valleys. Opposition troops then entered secret subterranean hideaways in the Malawa Valley for the first time. The ceilings were built from tree trunks packed with stone and dirt walls while the rock walls were several feet thick.

With opposition forces pushing their way from the north and Pakistani forces blocking the border to the south, the al-Qaeda fighters could only flee east or west over the mountains or fight their way out. Gary Berntsen, a key CIA commander involved in the fight against the Taliban around Kabul and the drive on Tora Bora, noted, 'Bin Laden split his force in two. One group, numbering 135 men, headed east into Pakistan . . . A number of al-Qaeda detainees later confirmed that bin Laden escaped with another group of two hundred Saudis and Yemenis by a more difficult eastern route over difficult snow-covered passes into the pashtun tribal area of Parachinar, Pakistan.

Three days later Commander Mohammad Zaman announced that his forces had attacked Spin Ghar itself at 0900 without any resistance. They came across fifty al-Qaeda dead and captured and one Arab fighter. Zaman claimed to have captured 80 per cent of the mountain. By the evening it was all over with the capture of another 35 al-Qaeda fighters and the discovery of about 200 dead. Among those captured was Mohamed Akram, who claimed to have been bin Laden's chef and who gave a good account of his boss's escape from Tora Bora.

Al-Qaeda suicide squads did not materialise. Despite exhortations to fight to the last, many of the dispirited defenders were buried by the bombardment, surrendered or just slipped away hoping to escape into Pakistan. Nonetheless, opposition commanders described the final battle as brutal, leaving the slopes of Tora Bora strewn with the bodies of al-Qaeda fighters.

Tora Bora turned out to be far from the impregnable fortress portrayed by the

Western media. A staff sergeant from the US Special Forces Operational Detachment Alpha 572 said afterwards:

> They weren't these crazy mazes or labyrinths of caves that they described. Most of them were natural caves. Some were supported with some pieces of wood maybe about the size of a 10-foot by 24-foot room, at the largest. They weren't real big. I know they made a spectacle out of that, and how are we going to be able to get into them? We worried about that too, because we see all these reports. Then it turns out, when you actually go up there, there's really just small bunkers, and a lot of different ammo storage is up there.

By mid-December al-Qaeda's supporters had been almost completely driven from the White Mountains. The speed of the victory came as a surprise to everyone. Zaman Gamsharik, opposition forces defence chief in eastern Afghanistan, announced on 16 December 2001, 'This is the last day of al-Qaeda in Afghanistan. We have done our duty we have cleansed our land of all al-Qaeda.' US Defense Secretary Donald Rumsfeld, visiting American forces at Bagram near Kabul, told them, 'The World Trade Center is still burning as we sit here. They are still bringing bodies out. Fortunately the caves and tunnels at Tora Bora are also burning.' Despite the victory at Tora Bora, Osama, perpetrator of the attacks on New York, had escaped capture.

In the aftermath of Tora Bora Pakistani security forces arrested at least 350 al-Qaeda members, including more than 300 Arab nationals (mainly Saudis, Sudanese, Egyptians, Jordanians and Yemenis), and most were transferred to the American detention facility Camp Rhino, at Kandahar. The number of foreigners remaining in the mountains was thought to be between 2,000 and 5,000, but scattered, cold and hungry they were not deemed a threat. By the end of the war the new Afghan government was holding about 7,000 prisoners. Around 100 of these were handed over to the US for further interrogation and another 900 were identified as being of potential interest to the US. About 350 Taliban and al-Qaeda prisoners were in American custody, some of whom were reportedly held at the US naval base at Guantanamo Bay, Cuba.

All that remained after Tora Bora was to mop up. Searchers also found heavy weapons, including one or two tanks, inside some of the caves. American forces examined the abandoned cave complexes in the Tora Bora region, where some believed bin Laden had been hiding. On the road to the Shah-i-Kot Valley, south-west of Tora Bora, reporters discovered a party of al-Qaeda fighters who said, 'The enemies of Islam have broken our backbone, our people are abandoning us and we have dispersed like orphans into the valleys.'

American reporter Philip Smucker was with the American forces and recalled:

Both of the caves I crept into resembled the portals of pharonic tombs I had entered a year earlier in Egypt's valley of the kings. The booty inside was not nearly as mesmerizing – only boxes upon boxes of Chinese anti-aircraft shells and Russian rockets, a few spent milk cartons, and a box of Cheerios. . . .

When we arrived back in Upper Pachir, a gaggle of Afghan children surrounded us . . . They laughed and shouted 'Osama, Osama Pakistan!' I think I knew what they were getting at, and I pointed across the snow capped Spin Ghar as they nodded and leapt in the air.

The involvement of the British SAS at Tora Bora and way to the south in the battle for the Taliban's opium stocks in Helmand province (under the codename Operation Trent) inevitably attracted speculative British media attention. It was not long before false rumours were spread by the British press that members of the SAS were in line for the Victoria Cross. Gallantry awards were received for this period but no VCs and the awards were credited to the individuals parent units not the SAS Regiment. The only VC received for action in Afghanistan was posthumous and was awarded in 2006 to Corporal Bryan James Budd of the Parachute Regiment.

An American CAS team and members of the Northern Alliance, west of Konduz, Afghanistan in late 2001. The man on the left is armed with a M4 Carbine, which includes the Carbine Special Operations Peculiar Modification Accessory Kit. Note the 'Technical' behind them, a truck mounting a 57mm anti-aircraft gun – while to the left the turret of a BMP armoured fighting vehicle is just visible. The Afghan fighter on the right is holding the ubiquitous rocket-propelled grenade.

The labyrinth-like compounds of the city of Kandahar, home of Mullah Omar and the Taliban – his movement spread from here in the mid-1990s to take control of Afghanistan in the wake of the chaos created by the Afghan civil war. In 2001 once the Taliban fled from the city they were expected to make a last stand at Tora Bora.

The Taliban quickly abandoned Herat, Kabul, Kandahar and Konduz and headed for the Pakistani border. These Taliban fighters hitching a lift in a Toyota pick-up are armed with assault rifles, a light machine gun and a RPG.

This parade of opposition fighters shows what a motley crew they were, although the Taliban were foolish to underestimate them. Many of these men had years of combat experience thanks to the interminable wars in Afghanistan.

The Tora Bora Valley in the Nangarhar province, south-eastern Afghanistan. In English this translates, as the Black Cave while the region was known locally as Spin Ghar or the White Mountains. Formed from limestone, the mountains are riddled with caves and these created small natural bunkers for the Taliban.

As a prelude to the Battle for Tora Bora Taliban positions were blasted by US Air Force B-52 bombers and Special Forces MC-130 Combat Talons. In particular the later was used to drop a Vietnam War-era Daisy Cutter on 9 December 2001. If the explosion itself did not kill you, the concussion would.

Looking like a nuclear explosion, this test detonation gives some impression of the power of the 15,000-pound BLU-82 Daisy Cutter bomb. This weapon was not retired until 2008.

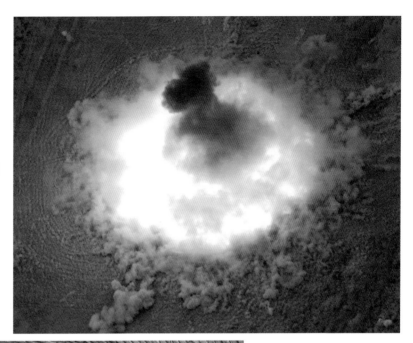

Tora Bora was found to be packed with aging Soviet and Chinese weaponry. This particular cache consisting of almost 900 boxes of Soviet rockets was stored in a cave at a former Soviet Union Training Camp north of Kandahar.

Following the capture of Tora Bora coalition forces set about systematically destroying the caves and the weapons they contained to prevent them ever being used again.

The escape of al-Qaeda's senior leadership contributed to the drone wars over Afghanistan and neighbouring Pakistan. The RQ-1 Predator unmanned aerial vehicle had been deployed in a reconnaissance role since the mid-1990s, but the armed version was not ready before 9/11. Uzbekistan did not grant the CIA permission to operate armed flights from its K2 airbase until 7 October 2001.

The Predator was followed by the much larger MQ-9 Reaper in 2007 which has the ability to carry both precision-guided bombs and missiles. The drone war escalated on both sides of the Afghan–Pakistani border.

The RQ-1 armed with an AGM-114 Hellfire missile was renamed the MQ-1 Predator. During September and October 2001 there were four unsuccessful attempts to ambush bin Laden. A Predator killed al-Qaeda's No. 3, Mohammed Atef (alias Abu Hafs), in November 2001 near Kabul. The following month a Predator destroyed a Range Rover believed to be carrying bin Laden. DNA samples later proved otherwise and this was the closest the MQ-1 got to killing him before he escaped from Tora Bora and into Pakistan.

Chapter Five

NATO Takes Charge

Mopping up operations continued well into the New Year, with the Coalition determined not to repeat the mistakes of the battle for Tora Bora. The next area to be subject to a search-and-destroy mission was the Sha-i-Kot Valley (also the scene of heavy fighting against the Soviet army in 1987).

Local defenders, while expecting renewed attacks from the Coalition, did not anticipate it happening so soon. In late February 2002 their strongholds were softened up by fighter-bombers, using 3,500 precision guided munitions, B-52H bombers dropping over 250 bombs and Hercules gunships spraying the area with gunfire.

On 2 March 2002, Operation Anaconda launched 1,200 American troops and 1,000 new Afghan government troops under General Zia Lodin against the Shah-i-Kot Valley, supported by an armada of warplanes. The key to the operation was to prevent al-Qaeda forces from fleeing into Pakistan, so heliborne assault troops were used to block the escape routes. However, Anaconda stirred up a hornet's nest. The column pushing up the valley road came under intense rocket and mortar fire and stalled, while one of the heliborne forces was accidentally landed in the midst of al-Qaeda defensive positions and suffered twenty-eight wounded. Air power proved crucial in helping clear the valley, though a further 1,000 Afghan government soldiers with armoured personnel carriers and tanks had to be called in. Few al-Qaeda dead were found and the enemy was either buried under the mountains or once again escaped.

Following Tora Bora and Anaconda, the American special forces conducted Operation Full Throttle on 14 June 2002, in the foothills of the Spin Ghar Mountains. This was in response to the Taliban regrouping north of Kandahar. Although Mullah Omar and bin Laden had gone to ground, these forces were thought to be under Mullah Akhtar Mohammed Osmani and Mullah Barader. In particular, Osmani – formerly the Taliban's 2nd Corps commander – had assumed the role of acting Taliban military chief in November 2001. Full Throttle was followed by Operation Anvil, which succeeded in capturing Osmani, but he subsequently escaped to Pakistan.

NATO assumed control of ISAF in 2003 and expanded its area of responsibility from Kabul to encompass the country's southern and eastern provinces three years later. This meant bringing the 12,000 American and other Coalition forces in the region under NATO control. It gave ISAF responsibility for the whole of Afghanistan, with around 40,000 troops. The upshot of this was greater integration in the south with the American-led Operation Enduring Freedom. However, the two operations continued to be directed separately, the rationale being that ISAF had a stabilisation and security mission, while OEF was overtly counter-terrorism.

While numerous countries provided contingents for peacekeeping in Afghanistan, the only notable numbers beyond Britain and the US were from Germany, Canada and the Netherlands. By early 2009 there were 56,420 foreign troops in Afghanistan of which 24,900 were American and 8,300 were British. The ANA totalled 79,300, though the Afghan government and UN agreed in 2008 to boost the ANA to 122,000 troops by 2011. It would eventually grow to 350,000.

The HQ of NATO's Allied Rapid Reaction Corps, under British direction, took control of ISAF in May 2006 for a nine-month period. This coincided with ISAF's move south and the arrival of additional British troops in Helmand province for three years. Taliban activities soon made it clear that British numbers and equipment were insufficient to contain the threat. This forced the British Ministry of Defence hurriedly to procure more armoured vehicles for deployment in Afghanistan during the first half of 2007.

The British public really woke up to the country's involvement when the 3 Para Battle Group deployed to Helmand province to help the Provincial Reconstruction Team (PRT) with security and stability in 2006. Sending just 3,000 men, of whom only a third were fighters supported by just six heavy lift helicopters, seemed over optimistic at best. This force would eventually expand threefold.

At the behest of the regional governor 3 Para found itself divided up into penny packets to bolster the wholly ineffective Afghan National Police and the ANA. The British platoon houses acted like honey pots attracting Taliban from around the province. The civilian PRT members were redundant in the face of an escalating ground war. Nevertheless, in Helmand and elsewhere bravery and tenacity coupled with superior NATO firepower soon persuaded the Taliban that they could not win a stand-up fight. Instead, they began to wage a brutal and effective Improvised Explosive Device (IED) campaign.

NATO-led ISAF was almost completely reliant on the goodwill and cooperation of neighbouring Pakistan. Around 75 per cent of all non-lethal supplies required by the 130,000 ISAF troops came via the Pakistani port of Karachi and were then trucked north. For this road traffic there were essentially just two key crossing points over the mountains between Afghanistan and Pakistan.

NATO-ISAF supply routes were highly vulnerable, a fact not missed by the Taliban. Convoys had little or no security and the Pakistani Police claimed that it was impossible for them to provide 24-hour protection. As a result, NATO civilian supply lorries were regularly targeted in Islamabad, Karachi, Peshawar and the southern province of Baluchistan from the summer of 2008 onwards. In the border areas the Taliban regularly hijacked lorries, kidnapped the drivers and stole their cargos. In the Khyber tribal region militants wrecked or seized numerous NATO transport vehicles.

American troops took considerable steps to secure Afghanistan's Kunar province to the north of the Khyber Pass. This was in response to insurgents filtering through the Pech and Kunar valleys towards Kabul. American Marine, Mountain and Airborne units established a string of bases in the Pech, Waygal, Shuryak, Chowkay and Korengal valleys. There were rumours that elements of the 9/11 attacks were planned in the Korengal. Similarly, there were rumours that both Osama bin Laden and Ayman al-Zawahiri used this route regularly to transit in and out of Pakistan. It was far easier to cut off ISAF's supply routes through Pakistan than to cut off the insurgents.

NATO and the US were highly critical of the Pakistani army's reluctance to tackle militants in North Waziristan following operations in South Waziristan. For some time both the US and NATO were demanding that Pakistan assert full control of all the tribal areas along the volatile Afghan border. It was here that foreign jihadists were trained to fight for al-Qaeda and the Afghan and Pakistani Taliban. In addition, North Waziristan provided sanctuary for militants conducting attacks right across Pakistan.

The Pakistani government came under increasing pressure from Washington to crack down on the unrest and lawlessness that was blighting supply convoys in the border regions. The different Pakistani militant groups, including the Taliban, had the ability to strike with seeming ease. Pakistan was like a powder keg, forever just one step from a spark that would blow the whole thing to pieces. The country was caught between a rock and a hard place. Its foreign allies and partners were constantly exhorting it to greater efforts in the war on terror both at home and abroad. Internally, its competing religious and political groups were constantly straining the very fabric of the beleaguered state.

In the meantime, the US and NATO were making rods for their own backs. The Taliban, normally largely dormant during the winter, escalated their campaign largely in response to US special forces conducting operations throughout the winter months against its leadership and logistical routes. In addition, missiles fired from US drones or unmanned aerial vehicles (principally the aptly named Reaper) regularly killed Afghan and Pakistani Taliban inside Pakistan. This created an anti-American backlash and culminated with tribal leaders in North Waziristan vowing revenge on the US.

In southern Pakistan the road runs from the city of Quetta to Chaman through the Khojak Pass and across the border up to Kanadahar, which sits astride Afghanistan's great ring road. To the north the road runs from Islamabad through Peshawar to the Khyber Pass and over the border to Jalalabad and on to Kabul.

Militants were able to cross the border via the innumerable mountain footpaths, many of which were developed during the Soviet-Afghan War.

The Taliban claimed they set up a special unit to target ISAF supply convoys inside Pakistan and that this strategy would not cease until the supply routes had been completely cut. The Taliban scored a notable propaganda coup when they filmed themselves with seized American Humvee motor vehicles in November 2008, which had been destined for American forces across the border in Afghanistan.

ISAF claimed its operations remained unaffected by the destruction of these vital supply convoys, but behind the scenes it was seeking alternatives in order to reduce its reliance on ever-unstable Pakistan. Clearly, ISAF could not sit idly by while the Taliban strangled it. However, the only real alternative was that supplies were brought into northern Afghanistan via Tajikistan and Uzbekistan. This was not a viable option, as all supplies first had to be flown in to intermediate countries rather than be shipped by sea.

In June 2010 around a dozen militants walked into a vehicle depot just 6 miles outside Islamabad and shot up twenty lorries setting them on fire. The attackers quickly escaped in two cars and on motorbikes, leaving behind millions of dollars worth of destruction and seven dead and four wounded. Alarmed at the complete lack of security, local truckers closed the grand trunk road between Lahore, Rawalpindi and Peshawar before the police managed to move them on. The Pakistani government refused to step up security despite the Taliban publicly acknowledging they were targeting the trucks and tankers. It was also alleged that Pakistan's intelligence and security forces were deliberately looking the other way to encourage the attacks to punish NATO for the border violations and American drone attacks.

Men of 45 Commando up in the Afghan mountains during Operation Jacana photographed on 17 April 2002. Despite their defeat, the Taliban remained a wily and troublesome adversary that required a whole series of mopping up operations. These included Buzzard and Jacana conducted by British forces.

A temporary Royal Marine forward operating base equipped with 105mm artillery and Milan anti-tank missiles photographed in April 2002.

This young marine is taking a break during Jacana – despite the men's high level of fitness the mountain slopes and altitude still made it very hard going. He is armed with the L86A1 Light Support Weapon, at 6kg it is a third heavier than the standard SA80 assault rifle. Each eight-man infantry section is normally equipped with two LSWs.

Men of 45 Commando being air lifted by a Chinook helicopter. This man is equipped with the British L7A2 General Purpose Machine Gun (GPMG) which has an effective range of 1,800m. As Operation Herrick, Britain's contribution to the counter-insurgency war, progressed the Royal Marines conducted their missions increasingly by helicopter. Such air assaults played to their tactical strengths.

A Royal Marine Commando stands on guard with his WMIK mounted GPMG as a Chinook prepares to 'dust off'.

A local gives this 45 Commando WMIK Land Rover Defender a cautious wave. Although unarmoured, these vehicles were able to lay down a heavy rate of fire and were actually liked by their crews as they offered 360-degree visibility. Many men were not so keen on being battened down inside the later range of armoured vehicles that were deployed to Afghanistan.

Moments such as this were always highly risky. The Taliban had a habit of engaging helicopters as they landed and took off with rocket-propelled grenades and heavy machine guns, while mortars, rockets and small-arms fire were always a threat to the landing zones which had to be constantly varied to stop the Taliban from exploiting operational habits.

Men from 45 Commando walking onto their air 'taxi'. As a result of the weight of their equipment and the danger of falling over, running either off or onto helicopters was completely out of the question. A fallen man would obstruct his comrades and present an immobile target for the Taliban.

A combat sapper from 59 Independent Commando Squadron Royal Engineers scours a Taliban hideout. Booby traps and abandoned ordnance always lurked to catch the unwary. Legacy mines left over from the Soviet-Afghan War posed a particular problem for coalition forces.

Another member of 59 Commando about to inspect a Taliban hideout.

Judging by the rubble, this cave suffered from the air raids. The Commando nearest the camera is armed with the L86A1 LSW, which is essentially a larger version of the British SA80 assault rifle. This weapon can fire single shot or fully automatic to a maximum range of 1,500m.

This member of 45 Commando photographed in 2002 is armed with the Minimi Para machine gun, a Belgian-designed weapon that is very popular with the world's special forces.

Another Taliban hideout is rendered inoperable.

American gunners from Alpha 37th Field Artillery fire an M119 Howitzer as part of a training exercise conducted near Kandahar airfield, Afghanistan on 17 September 2004. The M119 Howitzer is a lightweight 105mm towed weapon that is used to provide destructive, suppressive and protective indirect and direct field artillery fire.

A British WAH-64 Apache attack helicopter unleashes its rockets against a Taliban target. As the war progressed, British, American and Dutch Apaches provided vital close-air support for the ISAF ground forces. The British Army Air Corps first deployed in support of Task Force Helmand in 2006.

A close-up of the deadly M230 electrically operated Chain Gun that is the Apache's standard area weapon system. It can fire up to 625 rounds per minute, though the practical rate is half this with bursts of 10 rounds per second. The Apache also carries a mix of rockets and air-to-surface missiles.

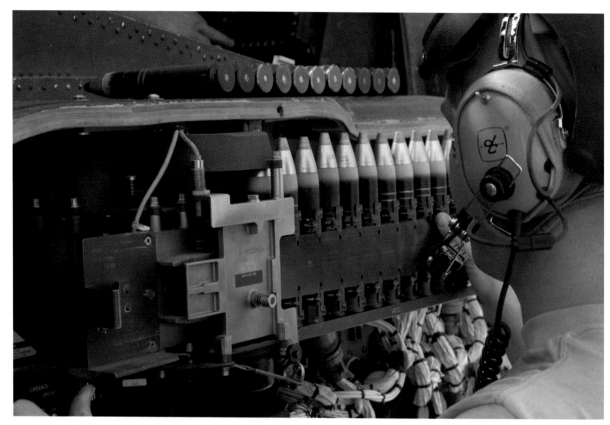

An American weapons technician loads M789 30mm rounds into an AH-64D Apache Longbow helicopter at Forward Operating Base Salerno in Khowst province on 19 April 2007. The helicopter is from the 82nd Aviation Brigade, US 82nd Infantry Division (Airborne) and can carry up to 1,200 30mm rounds.

British Apaches photographed at Camp Bastion.

Chapter Six

'Terry' Taliban

Although the Taliban was chased into the mountains of Afghanistan and neighbouring Pakistan, it was not long before they were regrouping. The Taliban goals were to oppose the extension of Kabul's rule, make the provinces ungovernable and drive the foreign troops out. The arrival of more and more ISAF troops in some instances alienated the locals, which meant a steady stream of recruits into the ranks of the Taliban-led insurgency and they were not happy at the presence of foreign troops on Afghan soil. To many illiterate and barely educated Afghans it seemed as if the bad old days of the Soviet invasion has returned. Yet another invader had to be repelled.

Essentially, there were a good dozen or so major opposition groups operating in Afghanistan, but they all tended to get lumped in together generically as 'Taliban'. The diehards opposing ISAF and President Karzai's government insisted on loyalty to the Taliban Quetta Shura and Mullah Omar. Key among these groups were the Taliban, the Haqqani network, Hezbe-e-Islami, the Pakistani Taliban and the Islamic Movement of Uzbekistan along with a number of Kashmiri separatist groups. Although predominantly Sunni, the insurgents were also drawn from the Shia and Sufi Muslim communities. The Haqqani network and Hezbe-e-Islami were old Mujahideen organisations that had fought the Soviets. In Helmand the British army found that the four main tribes were often at loggerheads – notably the Ishaqzai sided with the insurgents.

The Taliban excelled in classic guerrilla hit and run tactics that had been honed after three decades of continuous warfare in Afghanistan. Convoys and isolated outposts come under regular attack. In addition, the Taliban did not shy away from close-quarter combat and are experts in encirclement. In Helmand the British platoon houses became magnets for Taliban attacks. When 3 PARA arrived in Helmand they were under the misapprehension that they would be helping the regional reconstruction teams, instead they found themselves fighting a war. Often the insurgents would only withdraw when superior ISAF firepower forced them to do so. Analysis conducted for the US Marine Corps found that 'the Taliban tended to break contact when air support arrived – not because air strikes inflicted heavy casualties, but because air attacks made it too dangerous to continue fighting.'

There were essentially three tiers of Taliban – first, the hardcore Afghan fighters, then foreign jihadists come to fight holy war and finally the 'Ten Dollar' Taliban who were locals prepared to fight simply for money. The first two-tier fighters were rarely captured alive. Various drug warlords also had good reason to oppose the extension of rule from Kabul. This meant that Afghanistan's many tribes and local militias fluctuated in their loyalty.

As always in Afghanistan, there was no shortage of weapons. Rocket-propelled grenades and heavy machine guns posed the greatest threat to ISAF ground forces. As well as small arms, including assault rifles and light machine guns, the Taliban also fielded a range of heavier weapons that posed a potential threat to coalition aircraft. These included the old Soviet-designed SA-7 surface-to-air missile with a range of 4,000m and the Soviet-designed 14.5mm and 12.7mm heavy machine guns, which have effective ranges of 3,000m and 2,000m respectively. The latter had been used to great effect against Soviet helicopters during the Soviet-Afghan War.

The Taliban were also judged to have some of the newer SA-14 and Chinese HN15 SAMs, and even the odd US Stingers and British Blowpipe SAMs, but few if any were operable. There was only one high-profile attempt to shoot down an aircraft in Afghanistan using a SAM, but the threat remained forcing pilots to employ a wide range of counter-measures and evasive manoeuvres.

Taliban fighters typically did not wear any uniforms or ballistic protection in the shape of body armour or helmets – so they were not afforded any protection against gunfire, fragmenting rounds or ballistic pressure waves. This left them highly vulnerable to ballistic trauma and hydrostatic shock. What it also meant was that a fighter could quickly go from insurgent to local civilian by just stashing his weapon.

Battle Damage Assessment (BDA) following engagements with the Taliban was often hampered by the fact that they nearly always removed their dead and wounded from the battlefield. This made it difficult to confirm 'kills' and assess the effectiveness of the weaponry deployed. If all the insurgents were killed during an engagement then that was a different matter. This was typically the case with attack helicopters, which could remain on station hunting down every fighter using hi-tech sensors.

The Taliban provided little more than the most basic first aid to their wounded fighters. Removal of the dead from the battlefield is in part due to Muslim burial rites that dictate the deceased should be buried within 24 hours. The body should be washed and wrapped in cloth before burial. The Taliban knew it also hampered the enemy's BDA.

In Helmand and elsewhere, bravery and tenacity coupled with superior ISAF firepower soon persuaded the Taliban that they could not win a stand-up fight. Instead, they began slowly to wage a brutal and effective Improvised Explosive Device (IED) campaign.

It should be noted that 2011 was a particularly violent year. According to Human Rights Watch's 'World Report 2012: Afghanistan':

The armed conflict escalated in 2011. The Afghan NGO Security Office (ANSO) reported that opposition attacks increased to 40 a day in the first six months of the year, up 119 percent since 2009 and 42 percent since 2010. ANSO also reported a 73 percent increase since 2010 in attacks against aid workers, which included a fatal mob attack – sparked by the burning of the Koran by an American pastor in Florida – against a United Nations office in the city of Mazar-e-Sharif. Insurgent attacks reached previously secure areas including Parwan and Bamiyan as the war spread to many new parts of the country.

Civilian casualties rose again, with the UN Assistance Mission in Afghanistan (UNAMA) recording 1,462 conflict-related civilian deaths in the first six months of the year, a 15 percent increase since 2010. Some 80 percent were attributed to anti-government forces, most commonly caused by improvised explosive devices (IEDs).

In Helmand during 2010–11 only the three central districts of Nad-e Ali, Nahr-e-Saraj and Lashkar Gah were the responsibility of the British-led Task Force Helmand, the rest came under the US led-Task Force Leatherneck as Washington had decided to surge Helmand with the firepower of the US Marine Corps. These operations were met by the Taliban's spring campaign codenamed Badr (after one of the Prophet Mohammed's military victories). American resources inevitably meant that the weaker British forces became the centre of attention. In November 2011 it was announced that Nad-e Ali would be handed over to the Afghan security forces. Notably, insurgent activity did not readily recover after the winter lull of 2012 because of the level of military operations during 2011. Nonetheless, the Taliban and their allies remained far from defeated.

International Security Assistance Force Headquarters in Kabul. ISAF was created in accordance with the Bonn Conference in December 2001. NATO assumed leadership of the ISAF operation on 11 August 2003, ending the six-month national rotations. The Alliance became responsible for the command, coordination and planning of the force, including the provision of a force commander and headquarters on the ground in Afghanistan. ISAF's mandate was initially limited to providing security in and around Kabul. In October 2003, the United Nations extended ISAF's mandate to cover the whole of Afghanistan (United Nations Security Council Resolution 1510), paving the way for an expansion of the mission across the country.

Men of 45 Commando on patrol in the foothills of Afghanistan in the spring of 2002. Note the mixture of desert and jungle camouflage for their uniforms. At this stage, roadside bombs known as Improvised Explosive Devices were not a great threat.

More men from 45 Commando photographed during Operation Buzzard on 23 June 2002. They are test firing an enormous range of weaponry seized from the Taliban, which includes assault rifles, rocket-propelled grenades, heavy machine guns, mortars and an anti-aircraft gun.

Commandos tread carefully at an abandoned Taliban storage facility. There was a constant danger of booby traps or simply unstable munitions. The Taliban has vast caches of weapons stored across the country, much of it dating from the Soviet-Afghan War and the Afghan civil war.

Much of the weaponry and ammunition seized was not stored with any great care so was exposed to damp, varying humidity, dirt and dust. Stocks such as this were blown up on site as they were simply too dangerous to move.

French troops from the 1st Armored Company, setting up a heavy mortar inside Combat Outpost Dabo, Uzbeen Valley after receiving intelligence on possible insurgency attacks at the end of April 2009. The vehicle is a French VAB armoured personnel carrier.

A soldier from B Company, 1st Battalion, 32nd Infantry Regiment, US 10th Mountain Division patrolling the mountains near the village of Aranas in Nuristan province on 18 October 2006. This division played a key role in the war against the Taliban.

Another soldier from 1st Battalion, 32nd Infantry Regiment, US 10th Mountain Division engaging the Taliban with his M16 or M4 rifle in Barge Matal, in Afghanistan's eastern Nuristan province during Operation Mountain Fire, 12 July 2009.

More men from the US 10th Mountain Division engaging Taliban with their mortar during the same battle. Visible weapons include the M16A2 assault rifle and the M249 Squad Automatic Weapon.

ISAF-badged US soldiers of the 2nd Battalion, 327th Infantry Regiment, 101st Airborne Division during a firefight with Taliban forces in Barawala Kalay Valley in Kunar province, Afghanistan, 31 March 2011. Clearly, the Taliban had got round behind them. The man in the foreground is carrying a SAW.

Taliban fighters handing in their weapons during an ISAF-sponsored amnesty.

Romanian TAB-77 Armored Personnel Carriers assigned to Task Force Red Scorpion on patrol in Afghanistan in October 2002.

A Canadian Leopard tank is driven onto an American C-17 Globemaster III for transport to Kandahar on 17 October 2006. This was the first time since the Korean War that Canadian armour had seen action. Few tanks were deployed to Afghanistan – Canada and Denmark sent some Leopard 1 and 2 to support operations in the south-west. Notably, Danish tanks did sterling work supporting Task Force Helmand. In 2010 US Marine forces in the south-west were bolstered by about a dozen M1A1 Abram tanks.

Two photographs of the Romanian TABC-79 armoured personnel carrier deployed to Afghanistan, the one below is the medevac (medical evacuation) variant.

Chapter Seven

The IED War

It was the IED war that truly brought home the cost of involvement in Afghanistan. Be they pressure plate or remotely detonated bombs, they made vast areas of Afghanistan no-go areas. There were 304 recorded IED incidents in 2004, and staggeringly this number rose to over 10,000 in 2009 with most of them occurring in Helmand. The year before Helmand was redefined as a high-threat environment.

During 2006 and 2007 there were only two British bomb-disposal teams in Helmand because Iraq remained the main focus for IED disposal. The reality is that there were simply not enough Ammunition Technical Officers (ATO) to go round. However, in the space of two years Taliban IED attacks went up by a massive 300 per cent. Warrant Officer 2 Gary O'Donnell was the first ATO to be killed while trying to defuse an IED on 10 September 2008. He would not be the last.

One of the bloodiest periods of bomb disposal in the entire history of the British army occurred between August 2009 and March 2010, with the escalating loss of soldiers and ATOs due to the proliferation of IEDs. British soldiers were killed and injured on an almost daily basis. Alongside the ATOs, mounting numbers of American and Canadian bomb-disposal experts were also lost in southern Afghanistan to IEDs.

Then notably between March and October 2010 IED incidents were roughly the same as the previous seven months and intelligence indicated that NATO was winning the IED war. It seemed that the Taliban were reverting to more conventional means of attacking ISAF troops. Politically, this was far more acceptable as publicly it is better if a soldier is shot by the Taliban rather than blown up and maimed or killed.

A favourite trick of the Taliban was to combine large mortar rounds with 107mm rockets. They could also lay their hands on 122mm shells from the Soviet D-30 field gun. However, more modern shaped charges posed the biggest threat to NATO armoured vehicles. Reports indicated that Iran was supplying a mine known as the 'Dragon'.

The death of five soldiers from the Yorkshire Regiment and one from the Duke of Lancaster's Regiment, killed while travelling in a Warrior armoured fighting vehicle in March 2012, was a stark reminder of how mines and IEDs continued to blight military and civilian lives the length and breadth of Afghanistan.

Mines were sown with the aim of protecting major roads, air bases, military outposts and the main cities. They were also used to impede supply and escape routes through the mountains. While British families mourned the loss of loved ones, the question remained how did the Taliban manage to kill these soldiers when they were travelling in the safety of a Warrior?

A veteran workhorse, the Warrior first entered service with the British army in the late 1980s with final deliveries of an order of 790 by 1995. The Warrior was originally produced in six variants, all of which took part in Operation Desert Storm in 1991. Since then it has seen active service in the Balkans, Iraq and Afghanistan.

The Warrior has gone through a number of upgrades in its twenty-five-year career. Notably the combat dozer blade and the surface mine plough can be fitted to the Warrior. Due to operational security, the exact cause of the blast was not made public. Nonetheless, it was clear that this attack required considerable planning and a very large IED or anti-tank mine.

According to the HALO Trust (which specialises in removing hazardous war debris), since the late 1970s a staggering 640,000 mines were laid in Afghanistan, making it one of the most heavily mined places on the face of the earth. Mines were laid throughout the Soviet-Afghan War, during the Afghan civil war and during the conflict with the Taliban. Afghanistan remains littered with Soviet-era ordnance. The HALO Trust detects and destroys almost 100 tonnes of explosives every month. The British army first came into contact with legacy minefields at Kajaki Dam in 2006 with terrible results.

During the Soviet-Afghan War the Soviet army employed huge numbers of mines. For example, they laid 2 million anti-personnel mines in the mid-1980s in support of a single campaign. Key among them was the tiny PFM-1 'butterfly' mine, which was often dropped by helicopters onto supply routes.

The Mujahideen were also supplied with large quantities of a plastic anti-tank mine. Although not made in Italy, these were called 'Italian' mines by Soviet sappers. The guerrillas received so many of them they were known to use the explosives to fuel their stoves. The Pakistanis still manufacture anti-personnel mines and are believed to have a stockpile of some 6 million.

Since the late 1980s HALO has managed to destroy 761,063 mines in Afghanistan, of these 220,065 were emplaced mines that were largely cleared by hand and another 541,000 stockpiled mines. This, of course, was on top of NATO's efforts to counter the ever-present Taliban IED threat and thousands of mines remained in the ground. Under its Weapons and Ammunition Disposal programme, HALO has also overseen the deactivation of 2,800 artillery pieces and tanks as well as 50,000 light weapons. HALO also destroyed 10 million rounds of large-calibre ammunition and almost 50 million bullets. The task seemed endless.

The Mines Advisory Group (MAG) has assisted in mine clearance in Afghanistan through its work with the Organisation for Mine Clearance and Afghan Rehabilitation. MAG has also worked the other side of the border helping Pakistan.

The destruction of the Warrior and its crew came at a time when relations with Afghan President Hamid Karzai were fraught following the deaths of six American servicemen and thirty civilians in the wake of Korans being accidentally burned by American officials.

Local transport had to be constantly monitored to make sure it was not transporting weapons, explosives or illegal narcotics.

This gives some idea of the dangers faced by British, American and other ISAF forces. The Royal Marine is examining an assortment of different types of hand grenades and mortar or rocket rounds that look as if they have been made from rocket-propelled grenades.

US Marines from Company I, 3rd Battalion, 6th Marine Regiment in downtown Surobi on 23 May 2004. The battalion conducted security patrols and civil assistance operations throughout the region in support of Operation Enduring Freedom. These men are armed with the standard M16A2 assault rifle.

Men of the 2nd Marine Division Combat patrolling in a dry creek bed while searching caves in the Khowst area of Afghanistan in the summer of 2004. The terrain gives some idea of what they faced.

US Army soldiers patrol through the region of Nowabab, Afghanistan, on 7 October 2004. The soldiers are assigned to B Company, 1st Battalion, 505th Parachute Infantry Regiment. They are armed with the M4 carbine, essentially the M16A2 with a collapsible stock, and the M240 or M60 general purpose machine gun. By this stage the hunt for al-Qaeda leader Osama bin Laden had been largely abandoned.

An ISAF and Afghan National Army weapons haul in May 2008. It had been discovered near Shindand and contained machine guns, automatic rifles, cartridges, rockets, a launcher and grenades, anti-tank and anti-personnel mines, detonators and 5kg of explosives. All of this was ideal for insurgent attacks or creating deadly IEDs. The yellow plastic mine in the foreground was known as an 'Italian' mine, although this type did not come from Italy.

This enormous pile of ammunition, shells, mortar bombs and linked machine-gun bullets stacked near Kandahar shows the scale of the problem facing the ISAF Explosive Ordnance Disposal teams in Afghanistan. On 12 May 2005 American soldiers, Romanian soldiers and members of the British Royal Air Force were involved in a joint effort to demolish 10 tons of ordnance that was either confiscated during various cordon searches or belonged to coalition forces and was designated unusable. Essentially, the country was awash with weapons and ammunition.

Rockets and rusting ammunition covered in plastic explosives ready for destruction in late January 2005.

More Taliban ordnance is blown to smithereens. Explosive ordnance disposal Marines from Marine Wing Support Squadron 274 destroy an IED cache found by Marines from Lima Company, 3rd Battalion, 3rd Marine Regiment in an abandoned compound in southern Shorsurak, Helmand province during Operation New Dawn on 20 June 2010. Operation New Dawn was a joint operation between Marine Corps units and the Afghanistan National Army to disrupt enemy forces, which had been using the sparsely populated region between Marjah and Nawa as a safe haven. While patrolling the Marines found two directional fragmentation IEDs weighing 35 pounds each, 15ft of detonation cord and 15 pounds of ammonium nitrate and aluminium powder.

US Marines exit a suspect house in the Oruzgan Province on 28 April 2004. These men are from Charlie Company, Battalion Landing Team, 1st Battalion, 6th Marine Regiment. The battalion served as the ground combat element of the 22nd Marine Expeditionary Unit in Afghanistan conducting both combat and civil military operations.

Members of the US 82nd Airborne Division, Bravo Company 1/505 Parachute Infantry Regiment (PIR) enter a building during a combat raid on a village suspected of storing weapons on 16 October 2004 in Zurmat.

A British Commando prepares to destroy a Taliban drug haul.

A US Marine CH-53 flies over a large project site at the US Marine Corps home base Camp Leatherneck on 5 January 2011.

Chapter Eight

Tour of Duty

The number of international forces committed to ISAF paled into insignificance compared to the resources that Washington threw at the war with the resurgent Taliban. The lesson soon became apparent that to bring security ground needed to be cleared and then held to stop the Taliban infiltrating back. Numerous American forces served in Afghanistan, but at the start of OEF the key ones were the US 15th and 26th Marine Expeditionary Unit, US 10th Mountain Division and the US 101st Airborne Division who fought alongside the special forces. The ISAF regional commands were then bolstered by various infantry and mechanised units that included the US 1st, 2nd, 4th and 25th Infantry Divisions.

By 2002 there were around 7,000 American troops committed to OEF, and this swelled to 23,000 5 years later. At the end of 2009 as the war with the Taliban was escalating, President Obama ordered a surge of 30,000 who were deployed for the next 3 years. At this point the American military presence peaked at over 100,000 – keeping such vast forces in the field was an impossible feat for any nation other than the US. American forces also made up two-thirds of ISAF which accounted for around another 70,000 men and women.

While Britain's contribution to the war was much more modest, it clearly 'punched' well above its weight. The performance of 3 Commando Brigade during Operation Herrick 14 in the spring and summer of 2011 resulted in the British and American Forces Dining Club bestowing the brigade with a Historical Significance Award. This is given to outstanding units that have contributed to the UK-US alliance and set a benchmark.

In total 3 Commando Brigade conducted 41,000 patrols after taking over control of Task Force Helmand. The joint efforts of the Royal Marines of Task Force Helmand and US Marines of Task Force Leatherneck saw a 45 per cent reduction in violence in central Helmand in 2011. This was at the cost of nineteen British and forty-seven American personnel. In addition, over ninety British personnel were singled out for gallantry awards, commendations and recognition.

Before Herrick 14, 3 Commando Brigade had already made three previous deployments to Afghanistan. It first deployed in 2003 for Operation Jacana, then between September 2006 and April 2007 for Operation Herrick 5. During the next three six-month tours between April 2007 and September 2008 Herrick 6, 7 and 8 were conducted by British army brigades. 3 Commando Brigade then returned for Herrick 9, during which forty-two members were killed.

Elements of 3 Regiment, Army Air Corps equipped with the Apache attack helicopter served in Afghanistan from January 2011 to January 2012 as part of Task Force Jaguar and flew in support of Herrick 14. During this time Apache pilot Captain Antony Thompson was awarded a commendation by the Commanding General of the US Marine Corps 2nd Aircraft Wing for his skills and professionalism.

The British-built WAH-64 Apache first saw combat in Afghanistan. The Boeing AH-64 Apache attack helicopter was first introduced into US Army service in 1986. The AH-64D with the distinctive bulbous Longbow radar above the rotor blades appeared in 1997. It can operate in all weathers, day or night, and can detect, classify and prioritise up to 256 potential targets in a matter of seconds. The Apache has seen service in Afghanistan, Kosovo, Panama and during both Gulf Wars.

The WAH-64 is the UK AgustaWestland licence-built version of the AH-64D. There are two British Army Air Corps regiments (each with three squadrons) operating the WAH-64, which first deployed to Afghanistan on combat operations in 2006 in support of Task Force Helmand. They also deployed over Libya in 2011.

The 3rd Regiment AAC operated its Apaches in Afghanistan from January 2011 to January 2012, with its three squadrons each deploying on a four-month tour. 662 Squadron served first, then 663 followed by 653 Squadron who undertook their official handover on 20 September 2011. However, 653 did commence operations the week before. Notably, 662 Squadron is reported to have the highest 'kill rate' of any unit serving in Afghanistan. In Afghanistan the WAH-64 operated under the call sign 'Ugly' followed by a numerical designation, so Ugly 52 or Ugly 53, for example.

Afghanistan posed a particular set of problems as an operational environment that was exacerbated by IEDs and the geography. As a result, a vast range of military vehicles plied their trade with ISAF. Bearing the brunt of the European peacekeeping efforts were the wheeled French VAB and Panhard VBL, Finnish SISU, German Fuchs, Romanian TAB-79, Spanish BMR-600 and the British Saxon, which come in a variety of 4x4, 6x6 and 8x8 configurations. Tracked APCs included the French AMX-10, German Marder and Wiesel, Spanish Pizarro, Swedish CV9030, Turkish FMC-Nurol IFV and the British Warrior.

The Americans fielded the ubiquitous High Mobility Multipurpose Wheeled Vehicle (HMMWV) or Humvee, the tracked Bradley Infantry Fighting Vehicle and the wheeled Stryker, while the Canadians deployed the latter's cousin the wheeled LAV III and Bison. Operations in Iraq highlighted that many American military vehicles had inadequate protection. American convoys became the victims of increasingly aggressive IED attacks in the summer of 2003. This resulted in a massive upgrade programme costing $1.2 billion. The initial response on the ground was to use whatever was available in terms of plating to either weld or bolt onto the vehicles; some 4,500 vehicles received this treatment. Up-armoured Humvees were also redistributed to those units most in need.

The US 1st Cavalry Division began to add armoured layers to its vehicles before it left Kuwait for Iraq in April 2004 and by the end of the year over half of the division's Humvees were up-armoured, either through add-on-armour kits or as M1114s. Two battalions of the US 82nd Airborne Division were also equipped with new M1114s. The US was producing just 30 M1114s a month in 2003, but by the following year this had been ramped up to 400 a month and at the end of 2004 just under 6,000 up-armoured Humvees had been supplied.

The standard Canadian patrol vehicle for most missions in Kabul was the Iltis jeep, although soldiers complained about its lack of power, reliability and armour. German peacekeepers also use a similar vehicle, nicknamed the 'Dingo'. Audi designed the Iltis (or Ferret) for Volkswagen in the 1970s; Bombardier in Montreal took over production in the 1980s and manufactured it for the Canadian forces. Canada sought to replace the Iltis with a heavier Mercedes utility vehicle.

ISAF consisted of over 8,000 military personnel drawn from 36 nations. NATO assumed command in August 2003 and by 2005 Germany and France were the lead nations for the Kabul Multinational Brigade (KMNB), providing some 2,000 soldiers. The French Panhard VBL 4x4 reconnaissance vehicle and German Dingo were deployed to the streets of Kabul. The VBL went into production in 1990 and has also seen service in former Yugoslavia. The KMNB was responsible for the tactical command of all ground troops, whose vehicles remained vulnerable to Taliban attack. For example, an ISAF vehicle travelling in a six-vehicle convoy due north of Pol-e-Khomri was damaged in May 2005 by an explosion.

Following an attack on a German army bus in 2003, among the equipment the Germans deployed to Kabul was the tracked Wiesel air portable armoured weapon carrier. The extremely tough operating conditions in and around Kabul mean that the Wiesels took a severe battering, requiring some to be returned to Germany for refurbishment. The Danish army used Toyota VX 100 Landcruisers in Afghanistan as they provide a certain amount of protection against IEDs and small arms.

Perhaps appropriately enough, in light of its previous illustrious battle honours, the last unit to oversee the British withdrawal from Afghanistan and the end of Operation Herrick was the 7th Armoured Brigade. Better known as the 'Desert Rats', this brigade took over from the 1st Mechanised in the summer of 2013. This illustrious unit's heritage includes the battles fought in North Africa, Italy and Normandy during the Second World War and the Gulf in 1991 and 2003.

The Desert Rats arrived in Afghanistan with 6,000 men supported by some 300 armoured vehicles. While the 7th Armoured Brigade deployed with enough punch to take on the Taliban, the bulk of the force was made up of engineers and sappers whose job was to pack up. By this stage the British presence had shrunk from 130 bases to just 5 – the key of which was Camp Bastion. However you looked at it, this final tour of duty was essentially a rearguard action designed to ensure an orderly withdrawal.

A 45 Commando Royal Marine WMIK Land Rover on patrol in Afghanistan during Operation Buzzard/Jacana in late May 2002.

A 45 Commando convoy consisting of Land Rover Defenders and Pinzgauers. Such vehicles offered little protection against insurgent attack and led to various Urgent Operational Requirements for ballistic and mine-protected vehicles such as the Jackal and Foxhound.

A French Panhard Véhicule Blindé Léger (VBL, light armoured vehicle), 4x4 reconnaissance vehicle patrolling the streets of Kabul in support of ISAF. It went into production in 1990 and also saw service in former Yugoslavia.

While serving with ISAF, Belgian Army Pandur 6x6 APCs patrolling in Kabul in mid-September 2004. The purpose of the razor wire on the lead vehicle is unclear, though is probably simply a portable road block. The vehicle above is armed with the Belgian 7.62mm FN Mitrailleuse d'Appui Général, or GPMG, while the one below has the M2 .5in or 12.7mm heavy machine gun. Note the old Presidential Palace in the background.

A German Transporterpanzer or Fuchs APC at Kabul airport. German military transport has come under fatal attack in Afghanistan.

French soldiers from the 1st Armoured Company deploying a Véhicule de l'Avant Blindé or VAB (Armoured Vanguard Vehicle) east of Combat Outpost Dabo in the Uzbeen Valley of Afghanistan in early May 2009. The patrol searched caves in the cliffs in the valley to determine if insurgents were using them for weapons caches. The man nearest to the camera is armed with the French FAMAS assault rifle which entered service in 1980.

More French soldiers from the 1st Armoured Company in the Uzbeen Valley deployed as reinforcements for a forward scout team searching for insurgents reported to be in the area. The vehicle in the background is a VBL.

As part of Operation Slipper Australian Special Operations Task Groups' Long Range Patrol Vehicles drive in convoy across one of Afghanistan's desert, or 'dasht', regions in northern Oruzgan province on 10 October 2009. Such dust plumes could attract enemy mortar or rocket fire.

On patrol in north-east Bamyian with New Zealand's Kiwi Team One, performing both mounted and dismounted patrols, in July 2011. This man's personal weapon is an Austrian Steyr AUG (Armee Universal Gewehr – or Universal Army Rifle).

A VBL of the French 1st Airborne Hussars Regiment in Afghanistan in 2006.

A Romanian Army B33 (8X8) armoured personnel carrier leads a convoy of multi-national vehicles from Kandahar airfield to Kabul. The purpose of the convoy was to gather information and to help with a road reconstruction project during February 2002.

Coalition forces from Bulgaria drive an American-made up-armoured HMMWV in Kabul, Afghanistan, 28 July 2009.

A Task Force Warrior Mine Resistant Ambush Protected Vehicle and a Task Force Korrigan tactical armoured vehicle bring troops back to Combat Outpost Belda after they had completed a mission in Shpee Valley, Kapisa province in August 2009. The mission was part of a larger, three-day operation where three Afghan National Army companies, supported by 500 French marines with ISAF and Coalition force elements, conducted a large operation intended to deny the enemy safe haven and contribute to election security in Shpee.

A member of 51 Air Assault Squadron Royal Engineers surveying ISAF's Engineering Group HQ in Kabul. Behind him is a Russian-built BRDM-2 amphibious scout car belonging to the Afghan National Army.

Afghan National Army recruits in the ubiquitous Toyota pick-up. This vehicle was in widespread use with the Afghan National Security Forces but offered the occupants no protection whatsoever.

US Stryker armoured vehicles delivering humanitarian aid to the town of Rajan Kala on 5 December 2009. The Stryker is based on the LAV III light-armoured vehicle, in turn derived from the highly successful Swiss MOWAG Piranha III 8x8. The primary armament of the Stryker is a Protector M151 Remote Weapon Station with .50-cal M2 machine gun, 7.62 mm M240 machine gun or Mk-19 automatic grenade launcher. The 5th Brigade from the US 2nd Infantry Division became the first Stryker unit to deploy to Afghanistan as part of a troop level increase in the summer of 2009.

Chapter Nine

UOR – The Jackal

The Urgent Operational Requirements (UORs) thrown up by the British army's deployments to Afghanistan and Iraq resulted in the provision of a plethora of new military vehicles. Force protection became the primary focus for armoured vehicles, rather than the more traditional mechanised warfare role. While offensive battle groups still played their part, getting forces from A to B and conducting patrols unscathed in the face of a mounting IED threat became a greater priority. In total some 2,700 vehicles were supplied to the British army during the period November 2008 to April 2011 consisting of 18 different types.

UORs saw the successful provision of such force-protection vehicles as the Jackal, Mastiff and Ridgeback to the front line in Afghanistan, followed by the Panther and Springer. The Husky 4x4 and Wolfhound 6x6 were part of the deliveries, while the tracked Viking was replaced by the newer armoured Singaporean Kinetics Warthog. Notable among them was the Jackal, which provided off-road mobility, firepower and armoured protection for reconnaissance and convoy security duties. This served to complement and support the British army's fleet of Mastiff/Wolfhound 6x6 (US Force Protection's Cougar – British integration work was carried out in Coventry by NP Aerospace), the 6x6 Pinzgauer Vector (LPPV), Panther 4x4 command vehicle and the Husky 4x4.

The Ministry of Defence announced the purchase of 130 new weapons-mounted patrol vehicles in mid-2007 under an UOR for Iraq and Afghanistan. The Jackal 1 high-mobility weapons platform designed by Supacat and manufactured by Babcock/Devonport Management Ltd (DML) at their facility in Plymouth delivered a much-needed boost to the existing greatly maligned WMIK fleet (Weapons Mounted Installation Kit – initially installed on Land Rover Defenders), offering more firepower, a better range and crucially all-terrain mobility. The vehicle was fitted with a range of heavy firepower (including a .50 calibre machine gun or an automatic grenade launcher and a general purpose machine gun), as well as carrying a crew of four with their personal weapons.

Drawing on operational lessons, the £74 million follow-on order for about 110 state-of-the-art enhanced Jackal 2 and more than 70 Coyote Tactical Support

Vehicles was awarded to Supacat in early 2009. The latter is based on a 6x6 derivative of the Jackal. Both vehicles were bought as part of the Ministry of Defence's £700 million Protected Patrol Vehicles package. While Babcock secured the contract for the Jackal 1, Supacat was the prime contractor for the Jackal 2. The company has a long history of supplying military vehicles, but is perhaps best known for the compact Supacat 6x6 All-Terrain Mobility Platform (ATMP). This is now in its third generation with over 200 currently in service with the world's airborne and special forces.

In part thanks to the ATMP, Supacat has made itself a leader in high-mobility transporter technology. Its first customers for its High Mobility Transport vehicles (HMT – known as the 4x4 Jackal and 6x6 Coyote in British service) were the world's special forces. Operational requirements in Afghanistan soon meant that it filled a much wider capability gap. While Jackal 1 was essentially the HMT 4x4 with bolt-on armour and an armoured bathtub arrangement for the driver compartment providing protection against mine and IED blasts, Jackal 2 evolved increasingly into a true armoured vehicle with much of the armour as an integral part of the vehicle itself. Additional steel plating protects the passenger seats. The upgrade also saw engine enhancements that pushed its gross weight up to 7.6 tons. To ensure a 360-degree fire arc for the main armament the weapons cupola was raised.

Jackal 2, with its bigger engine, an extra body length of 14in and an extra crew seat, was a much better vehicle than its predecessor and was aimed at providing extra space for much-needed equipment. Speed was important in Afghanistan and with its 6.7 litre Cummins engine (replacing a 5.9 litre) and top speed of 80mph (130km/h) on roads and 55mph (90km/h) cross-country it ensured that it had a better chance of dealing with trouble at its own pace, quickly and effectively.

With the Afghan National Security Forces (ANSF) having assumed responsibility for security across the country in 2013 there was concern about what would be left behind. The British armed forces had 137 bases; in central Helmand by this stage there were just 13. In addition, British troop levels were reduced from 7,900 to 5,200 as Task Force Helmand slowly wound down. British Forces HQ in Afghanistan relocated from Lashkar Gah to Camp Bastion. Task Force Helmand had been based at Lashkar Gah since 2006 when Britain first increased its involvement.

There was speculation that many of the vehicles procured under UORs might be abandoned or gifted to the Afghan army. Many of them were acquired to meet particular operational conditions, not least to provide protection in the unending war against Taliban IEDs. This idea was not taken up by the Ministry of Defence and 99 per cent of vehicles were to be returned to Britain.

As a result, an £11 million site was established in Afghanistan to process equipment ready for its homeward journey. Vehicles such as the Coyote, Foxhound,

Husky, Jackal, Mastiff and Panther all have to be bio-washed in a process that can take up to 24 hours. According to the Ministry of Defence's Defence Equipment and Support organisation, once this process was completed 2,700 vehicles were returned – 200 more than announced to Parliament. In early 2013 Lord Astor told the House of Commons that the Ministry of Defence was seeking to recover around £4 billion of inventory, the equivalent of 6,500 20ft containers and about 2,500 vehicles. On top of this, 400 tonnes of brass cartridge cases and 100 pallets of ammunition were retrieved. Likewise, 300 tonnes of lithium batteries were salvaged.

Constant instability in neighbouring Pakistan meant that the Ministry of Defence could not rely on the southern transit route to Karachi and the Arabian Sea, so sought to secure a northern line of communication through the Central Asian republics and Russia. After much horse-trading, which involved gifting surplus British equipment, three transit agreements were reached with Uzbekistan. These allowed the movement of non-warlike stores and motorised armoured vehicles by rail as well as the movement of war-like stores and personnel by air. In return Uzbekistan got surplus Leyland DAF trucks and Land Rover spares after it was decided they were unlikely to be used for human-rights violations or internal repression.

Despite all this activity, Britain's commitment to Afghanistan's security continued. In October 2013 7th Armoured Brigade assumed responsibility for Task Force Helmand under Operation Herrick 19.

British Military Vehicle Deliveries

90 CVR(T), Coyote and Springer	August 2009
119 Husky, Mastiff, Jackal and Vixen	September 2009
81 CVR(T), Husky and Jackal	October 2009
66 Jackal, Ridgeback and Vixen	November 2009
105 Jackal, Wolfhound and Vixen	December 2009
222 Jackal, WMIK and Wolfhound	January 2010
260 Husky, Jackal, Mastiff, Wolfhound and Vixen	February 2010

Supacat's Jackal 2 in all its glory represents over 7 tons of armoured reconnaissance vehicle; note the vital V-shaped hull at the front designed to reflect mine or IED blasts away from the crew. Armoured plates on the sides also offer the occupants some protection from small arms. The ability of the Jackal 1 and 2 to tackle almost any terrain meant that the vehicle soon won favour with British troops serving in Afghanistan.

The earlier Jackal 1 on patrol. Reminiscent of Second World War long-range desert group vehicles, it can get into and out of trouble very quickly. The immediate and obvious difference between Jackal 1 and 2 is the raised weapons cupola on the latter, which allows a 360-degree arc of fire without deafening the driver. Note the large armoured doors in the middle; spare wheels are carried on the inside of these. Smoke dispenser tubes are mounted fore and aft.

45 Commando Pinzgauer and Land Rover WMIKs on patrol in Afghanistan. Although visibility was good, these vehicles left the crews highly vulnerable to IEDs, rocket-propelled grenades and small-arms fire.

US Marine Corps Major General Richard P. Mills, the commander of Regional Command Southwest, en route to Maiwand, Afghanistan in a Coyote 6x6 on 26 January 2011. This trip was followed by a visit to Lashkar Gah in Helmand to see Govenor Gulab Mangal.

Factory fresh, the Coyote is essentially a 6x6 derivative of the Jackal.

45 Commando WMIKs photographed during Operation Buzzard/Jacana in May 2002. This shows just how exposed the driver and gunner were.

Another vehicle born from the operational requirements of Afghanistan was the Light Protected Patrol Vehicle, or LPPV. It was dubbed the Foxhound by the British army and this was one is at Camp Bastion in mid-2012.

The Foxhound being put through its paces in Afghanistan – this vehicle was initially known as the Ocelot before joining the British army. Like the Jackal, its hull tapers out to deflect mines and IEDs away from the crew compartment.

This is a Husky Protected Support Vehicle deployed with the 1st Mechanised Brigade in late January 2013. Once again this was born from the British army's operational requirements in Afghanistan and Helmand province in particular.

British servicemen with B Flight, 27 Squadron, Royal Air Force Regiment stop on a road while conducting a combat mission near Kandahar airfield, Afghanistan on 2 January 2010. The vehicle is a Defender WMIK.

An up-armoured Humvee on patrol in Afghanistan.

Another Hummer on patrol at Kabul international airport in September 20111.

The American 6x6 Cougar mine-resistant infantry mobility vehicle. Depending on its configuration it is known as the Mastiff and the Wolfhound protected patrol vehicles in British army service. The British also used the 4x4 version dubbed the Ridgeback.

A British tracked BvS 10 Viking of the Queen's Royal Lancers, Viking Group traversing the Afghan desert in Helmand in 2008. The armoured amphibious vehicle is a larger cousin of the earlier Bv 206. The Viking first went into service with the Royal Marines in 2005 and was deployed to Afghanistan the following year.

Chapter Ten

Shouldering the Burden

Prior to NATO's withdrawal in 2014 ISAF had its work cut out ensuring that the transition ran according to plan. Likewise, ISAF acted to ensure its withdrawal was a dignified affair and that the government in Kabul was left firmly in control of the country. ISAF's regional commands slowly handed over their security mission hoping that there was no major rollback to the Taliban of those areas formerly under its control.

The beginning of the end for the NATO-led ISAF mission and OEF was marked on 18 June 2013. NATO handed over control of combat operations to the ANSF, which meant they had to take the operational lead in all 34 of Afghanistan's provinces covering 403 districts. The Afghan army has half a dozen corps commands, key among these are the 201 in Kabul, 205 in Kandahar and 215 in Lashkar Gah. The twelve-year war was finally winding down or at least for the international community and the NATO allies.

However, in mid-2013 there were still 100,000 troops from 50 countries in Afghanistan, and of these 68,000 were from the US and 8,000 from Britain. While it may have partially solved its manpower problems, a question remained over the ANA's capabilities and indeed competency. Did it have the resources and abilities to tackle the Taliban head on? Afghan government forces will particularly miss ISAF firepower, air support, most notably air strikes and transport helicopters.

Worryingly, the ANSF has grown from 40,000 to 350,000 in the space of just over 3 years. At such an accelerated rate of expansion it is hard to see how the ANSF can maintain its cohesion and be managed effectively. Although the ANA and ANP have around 350,000 men under arms, what happens after the coalition's departure and financial backing diminishes is an unanswerable question.

ANA and ANP attrition rates mean that they need 50,000 new recruits every year, which is clearly unsustainable in the long term. In addition, highly truncated training schedules did not help with the quality and competency of the recruits either. The elite 10,000-strong special forces, including 333 Commando unit, are better equipped, better paid and motivated. However, they cannot be everywhere at once. In Afghanistan it is a case of fear the worst and hope for the best.

While the US envisaged the ANA numbering at least ¼ million troops, by the end of 2011 it had reached about 180,000 according to the Afghan Ministry of Defence. Sceptics argued that the figure was nearer 100,000 – effectively 10 divisions to maintain order across a country the size of Afghanistan. The ANSF totalled 140,000 in 2008, but by March 2012 had reached 330,000 with a goal of 352,000 by late 2012. These figures seemed overly optimistic. The ANA has been plagued by problems. Maintaining, never mind boosting, manpower levels has been hampered by desertion – at one stage this was up to 2,000 men a month.

In the summer of 2012 an optimistic Armed Forces Minister Nick Harvey stated:

> The ANSF are on target to reach their maximum 'surge' size of 352,000 by November 2012, and are being equipped to support that number. Beyond 2014 the focus will be on sustainment and NATO is giving increasing emphasis to the enabling functions necessary to ensure the self sufficiency of the forces as they get ready to take full responsibility for security across the country.

Training was hampered by only just over 10 per cent of recruits being literate. Drug use was also a common problem with at least half of all soldiers using illegal substances. Loyalty has often been an issue, with instructors regularly removing mobile phones from ANA recruits due to lax tactical security. Small-arms discipline and accuracy was lamentably poor. It was difficult weaning the ANA off the old tactic of 'spray and prey' when firing their small arms or insisting on releasing a deluge of hot metal every time a firefight breaks out.

Members of the NATO Operational Mentor and Liaison Teams (OMLT) often despaired of the conduct of the ANA and ANP. In the early days some OMLTs often found it easier to conduct operations themselves rather than try and direct their Afghan students when faced by a real situation. This leading from the front meant that the OMLTs shouldered the burden of the fighting.

From 2006 all major operations in Helmand province were spearheaded by British or American troops. From the spring of 2009 the Afghan army escalated its small independent operations to larger scale ones, but it is never clear how much the ANA and ANP were simply providing window dressing to NATO-backed offensives against the Taliban. Most hope rested with the ANA's quick reaction forces, which consist of seven QRF battalions organised as motorised infantry equipped with Guardian armoured security vehicles. The first such battalion was supposed to be operational by the spring of 2012. There is also a Special Operations Command in charge of the ANA Commando Brigade and the ANA Special Forces.

As in Iraq, Washington has attempted to wean local forces off their reliance on the long-serving AK-47 Kalashnikov assault rifle. From 2008 onwards the Americans began replacing the ANA's AK-47s with American-supplied M16 rifles and M4 carbines.

The Afghan government worked to end the country's reliance on private Western security firms who provide protection for infrastructure projects. This was part of the overall transition to Afghan-led security. In the summer of 2010 President Hamid Karzai instructed that employing private security companies should stop and this function be taken over by the Afghan Public Protection Force (APPF). This assumed responsibility for the security of commercial businesses, development projects and convoys that need guarding. The intention was that private security guards join the APPF under whose auspices they would then be contracted to clients that require their services.

Following the launch of Operation Enduring Freedom and the steady military build-up, the international community has worked hard to foster institutions in Afghanistan that are conducive to unity and democracy. The country has endured over three decades of bloodshed and most Afghans want peace. However, the Taliban have retained the ability to erode much of the progress that has been made.

Osama bin Laden, leader of al-Qaeda, was killed on 2 May 2011, not in Afghanistan but in Pakistan by US Special Forces SEAL Team Six. This ended the rationale for Operation Enduring Freedom and set in motion ISAF'S withdrawal in 2014, ending over a decade of conflict.

With the assistance of ISAF it fell to President Hamid Karzai to prepare the Afghan National Security Forces, in the shape of the National Afghan Army and the Afghan National Police, to take on the security burden when NATO relinquished its mission.

Throughout the war in Afghanistan cooperation with local forces was very much the focus. In the summer of 2008 3 PARA deployed to Kandahar city to assist the ANSF. Located within the city football stadium, elements of 3 PARA carried out regular foot patrols around the inner city area side by side with the ANP.

A British soldier inspecting ANP checkpoints along the road from Camp Bastion to the west of Helmand province in 2008. Initially, many of the operational mentoring and liaison teams found themselves doing much of the fighting but as the situation stabilised they were able to focus more on their mentoring role.

Pictured on the right, a German soldier with the ISAF German Operational Mentor and Liaison Team Six patrols the streets of Mazar-e-Sharif with Afghan soldiers from the 2nd Kandak, 1st Brigade, 209th Corps, Afghan National Army on 11 February 2009. The OMLTs did a vital job in bolstering the confidence and professionalism of Afghan government forces.

A British soldier, along with his ANA counterparts, pauses during Operation Aabi Toorah which took place against the Taliban in central Helmand in March 2009. Rather than the Kalashnikov, these Afghans are armed with the American M16.

Members of the Afghanistan National Army lay out razor wire as a deterrent in an area just south of Combat Outpost Dabo in the Uzbeen Valley on 30 April 2009. These men are armed with the Egyptian-produced Madi Misr assault rifle – a clone of the Russian AKM.

Marines from Alpha Company, Battalion Landing Team 1st Battalion, 6th Marines startle the owner of a compound who refused to open his door for a search during Operation El Dorado in 2005. BLT 1/6 is the ground combat element of the 22nd Marine Expeditionary Unit (Special Operations Capable).

Afghan National Army gunners setting up their D-30 122mm howitzer. Such fire-support missions became ever more important as NATO/ISAF withdrew its military commitment.

More Afghan troops under German tuition on the streets of Mazar-e-Sharif in February 2009.

Afghan National Army recruits at the Kabul Military Training Centre in 2007. ANA numbers had to expand at a rapid rate as Kabul assumed control from ISAF for the provinces.

More ANA recruits armed with Romanian-produced Kalashnikovs. Men like these took full responsibility for their country's security and stability in 2014 when the ISAF mission came to an end.

It fell to Afghan President Hamid Karzai to oversee the difficult transition period. He often had to tread a fine line when it came to giving foreign troops a free hand without alienating his own people.

Shouldering the burden.

Epilogue

All wars are the same in that they are about killing and prevailing against an enemy. Yet all wars are unique as they are fought under different political and military circumstances, different environments and the conflict and weaponry evolves as it is pursued to an outcome. One model does not fit all. Indeed, the aftermath of all wars is different.

The conflicts fought in Vietnam, the Balkans and Iraq provided vital lessons for politicians and military strategists. Certainly the war in Afghanistan has much in common with Vietnam except the dense jungle was substituted for mountains. Inevitably, the moral question of whether Operation Enduring Freedom fought to oust al-Qaeda and drive the Taliban from power in Afghanistan was the right thing to do dominates perceptions of the successes and failures of the campaign.

Nevertheless, the international intervention in Afghanistan was in many ways a unique operation. While the application of air power and special forces brought the Taliban down, Coalition ground troops were needed to keep the resurgent Taliban at bay and safeguard the fledgling democratic government in Kabul. Like the Balkans Wars of the 1990s, Afghanistan became an unwelcome and often unpopular open-ended military commitment that dragged on for over a decade. As with the war in Bosnia, the campaign in Afghanistan only achieved a precarious peace after more and more ground troops were sucked in.

Elements of the Afghan War bear striking similarities with the Vietnam War. Like the 'Vietnamisation' process during the Vietnam War, it took far too long to get the new ANSF up and running. As in the case of Vietnam, it meant that foreign troops had to endure the brunt of the fighting while indigenous forces were recruited, trained and brought up to strength ready for a hand over of security operations. In turn, it meant that time and resources were expended fighting the enemy instead of concentrating on building up the ANA.

This mirrored the problems faced by the Army of the Republic of Vietnam – ARVN was not ready to shoulder the burden in South Vietnam and this nearly ended in disaster in the late 1960s. In Vietnam the American military had to conduct and oversee much of the fighting. The similarities do not end there. In the case of the Vietnam War American forces were never able completely to defeat the Viet Cong and their North Vietnamese backers; in Afghanistan the international coalition was never able completely to defeat the Taliban and their Pakistani tribal allies. Both wars ended in unwanted compromises.

What was originally intended as purely a security mission soon expanded to encompass the war on drugs with ill-fated attempts at eradicating the poppy harvest. Unfortunately, Afghans found it hard to pass on such a lucrative cash crop. To be fair the UN struggled for decades trying to find a way to keep Afghanistan's opium and heroin off the streets in the West and all its inducements and incentives always stumbled. Attempts were made to help Afghanistan develop a functioning democratic process with free and open elections. Central government was expanded out from Kabul into the provinces along with a functioning police force and military. Likewise, improving education for both males and females was championed as well enhancing and safeguarding women's rights. While Operation Enduring Freedom did not get Afghanistan completely back on its feet, it certainly made progress in many areas.

Suggested Further Reading

Beattie MC, Doug, *An Ordinary Soldier Afghanistan: A ferocious Enemy. A Bloody Conflict. One Man's Impossible Mission*, London, Pocket Books, 2009

Beattie MC, Doug, *Task Force Helmand A Soldier's Story of Life, Death and Combat on the Afghan Front Line*, London, Simon & Schuster, 2009

Berntsen, Gary and Ralph Pezzullo, *Jawbreaker The Attack on Bin Laden and Al-Qaeda: A personal Account by the CIA's Key Field Commander*, New York, Crown Publishers, 2005

Bishop, Patrick, *Ground Truth*, London, Harper Press, 2009

Bishop, Patrick, *3PARA*, London, Harper Perennial, 2010

Coll, Steve, *Ghost Wars The Secret History of the CIA, Afghanistan and Bin Laden, from the Soviet Invasion to September 10, 2001*, London, Penguin Books, 2005

Duncan DFC, Light Lieutenant Alex 'Frenchie', *Sweating the Metal*, London, Hodder & Stoughton, 2011

Flynn CGC MC, Mick, *Trigger Time*, London, Orion Books, 2011

Grahame, Sergeant Paul 'Bomber' and Damien Lewis, *Fire Strike 7/9*, London, Ebury Press, 2011

Kemp, Colonel Richard and Chris Hughes, *Attack State Red*, London, Penguin, 2010

Kiley, Sam, *Desperate Glory At War in Helmand with Britain's 16 Air Assault Brigade*, London, Bloomsbury, 2009

Lewis, Damien, *Apache Dawn*, London, Sphere, 2009

McNab, Andy (ed.), *Spoken from the Front Real Voices from the Battlefields of Afghanistan*, London, Corgi Books, 2010

Macy, Ed, *Apache*, London, Harper Press, 2008

Moore, Robin, *Task Force Dagger The Inside Story of Special Operation Forces in the War on Terror*, London, Macmillan, 2003

Rayment, Sean, *Bomb Hunters In Afghanistan with Britain's Elite Bomb Disposal Unit*, London, Collins, 2011

Southby-Tailyour, Ewen, *3 Commando Brigade Helmand Assault*, London, Ebury Press, 2011

Steele, Jonathan, *Ghosts of Afghanistan The Haunted Battleground*, London, Portobello Books, 2011

Townsend, Mark, *Point Man*, London, Faber & Faber Ltd, 2013